LIBRARY MANAGEMENT
TIPS THAT WORK

LIBRARY MANAGEMENT TIPS THAT WORK

Carol Smallwood, editor

AMERICAN LIBRARY ASSOCIATION
CHICAGO   2011

Carol Smallwood received her MLS from Western Michigan University and her MA in history from Eastern Michigan University. *Writing and Publishing: The Librarian's Handbook* and *Librarians as Community Partners: An Outreach Handbook* are 2010 ALA anthologies she has edited. *Lily's Odyssey* and *Contemporary American Women: Our Defining Passages* are new releases outside librarianship. Her magazine credits include *The Writer's Chronicle*, *English Journal*, and *Michigan Feminist Studies*; her library experience covers work in school, public, academic, and special libraries as well as being an administrator and consultant. This is her twenty-fourth published book.

Printed in the United States of America
15 14 13 12 11   5 4 3 2 1

While extensive effort has gone into ensuring the reliability of the information in this book, the publisher makes no warranty, express or implied, with respect to the material contained herein.

ISBNs: 978-0-8389-1121-1 (paper); 978-0-8389-9286-9 (PDF); 978-0-8389- 9287-6 (ePub); 978-0-8389-9288-3 (Mobipocket); 978-0-8389-9289-0 (Kindle). For more information on digital formats, visit the ALA Store at www.alastore.ala.org and select eEditions.

Library of Congress Cataloging-in-Publication Data
  Library management tips that work / Carol Smallwood, editor.
     p. cm.
  Includes bibliographical references and index.
  ISBN 978-0-8389-1121-1 (alk. paper)
  1. Library administration–Handbooks, manuals, etc. I. Smallwood, Carol, 1939-
  Z678.L4858 2011
  025.1–dc23
                                                                    2011017081

Book design in Din and Electra by Casey Bayer.
Cover image © Thomas M. Perkins/Shutterstock, Inc.

⊚ This paper meets the requirements of ANSI/NISO Z39.48–1992 (Permanence of Paper).

*My thanks to Mary Lou Andrews
for technical help online.*

CONTENTS

PART III   INFORMATION TECHNOLOGY

PART IV   STAFF

PART V   PUBLIC RELATIONS

FOREWORD

THE DIVERSITY of topics covered in this book attests to the broad scope of responsibilities that managing libraries requires. Managers must prepare their buildings and staffs for disasters, set standards and enforce rules, and trust their staff members to have the judgment necessary to get the work done on a daily basis. One major theme of this book is that managers of libraries do so much more than approve payroll and build collections, especially when personnel is limited.

All of these aspects and more must be considered in order to operate a library with unique local circumstances while continuing to build rapport with the community. As Lynn Hawkins, executive director of Mentor (Ohio) Public Library writes, libraries and library managers have "long arms" that must embrace an even longer list of responsibilities. Different management styles are required for overall success, which is why supervisors should also be enablers. They should enable their library's patrons to be proactive with their own needs, and they should enable their staff to reach out with their own powerful "long arms" to provide innovative and entrepreneurial means of assisting patrons.

The experiences of this volume's contributors are proven ways of achieving goals. Chapters discuss the all-important role of communication, how to work with boards, ways to capitalize on resources at hand such as volunteers, creating and fostering partnerships, and how to merge service points—which is more than a current trend; it is a new standard that libraries face because their budgets cannot support enough staff to maintain different service desks. Other chapters relate plans for engaging students and patrons, taking advantage of open-source information technology to assist with management goals, and coaxing still more work out of employees, along with even more best practices for handling public relations and marketing.

Although libraries are in the business of providing customers with information and services as a kind of product, business models do not speak to the intricacies involved with running a library. After reading this book, we see the nuances of models and segments of styles that library managers seem to adopt instinctively.

Among their many roles, libraries are community centers, gathering spaces, academic pivot points, harbors, workspaces, learning centers, computing centers, publicity firms, and technology hubs. That librarians become managers without the formal education of business majors speaks to the entrepreneurial, adaptive, motivated spirit of people who work in libraries. Librarians know that success is measured not by the value of stocks and bonds but by the quality of services provided and by the gratitude shown by patrons.

Management responsibilities often come to librarians in difficult times, as when budgets forbid new hires, when blended librarianship is the norm, when young librarians are thrust into leadership positions without the leisure of gaining experience by rising through the ranks, and when new generations of technology dictate a new paradigm for the administration and role of libraries. As long as anthologies such as this document how we accomplish our work in these changing times, people in management positions will be ready to meet the needs of communities.

—**Melissa J. Clapp, George A. Smathers Libraries, University of Florida**

PREFACE

LIBRARY MANAGEMENT TIPS THAT WORK is an anthology for public, academic, special, and school librarians looking for successful examples of management when so much is changing in the profession: how to manage staff, time, boards, emergencies, finances, stress, patrons, technology, and related topics day after day with budget and staff cuts. It provides guidance on planning as well as execution. Managers are sometimes defined as those who bring out the best in others; in the library it is a term not limited to directors but includes youth services coordinators, reader advisors, web administrators, and circulation heads, any of whom could be in small rural libraries or large urban settings. This collection is for beginners as well as old hands, and for solo librarians and those part of a large staff. It includes chapters centered on practical results by librarians making hard choices to provide the best service, whether that be one of the library's many specialized services or activities more commonly associated with library directors.

Management is central to good libraries, no matter the type of library or the librarian's position title and roles, but it is largely learn-as-you-go, as expressed by the librarians who generously share their experiences in this volume. You may have had management classes, read books on management style, and attended workshops and webinars filled with well-designed organization charts, but these chapters will provide valuable insight on how influential managers really are—and on what they can do to make that influence work for the library and its patrons.

For this collection, I sought chapters from practicing public, school, academic, and special librarians from different areas in the country. I asked contributors to write concise, how-to case studies of successful managers employing innovation. Some suggested topics in the call were staff flex hours, financial planning, administrative skills, public relations, time management, library boards, partnering, library manuals, professional ethics, innovative technology, handling employees, and volunteers.

It was my privilege to work with the librarians willing to share their experiences. These dedicated and creative professionals illustrate many facets of what makes an effective library manager—what really works in these challenging times.

Carol Smallwood

ACKNOWLEDGMENTS

Edgar Bailey, former Library Director, Providence College Library

George Bergstrom, contributor, *The Frugal Librarian: Thriving in Tough Economic Times* (ALA Editions, 2011)

Emily Dill, Associate Librarian, University Library of Columbus, Columbus, Indiana

Mary Dugan, Asst. Prof. of Library Science and the Resource Development Librarian in the Management and Economics Library at Purdue University

Carol Luers Eyman, Outreach and Community Services Coordinator, Nashua Public Library, Nashua, New Hampshire

Leslie Farison, Business Librarian and Assistant Professor at Appalachian State University, Boone, North Carolina

Elizabeth Goldman, CEO, Perth & District Union Public Library, Perth, Ontario, Canada

Ken Johnson, Coordinator of Learning & Research Services, Appalachian State University

Mary Laskowski, Head of Information Processing & Management, University Library, University of Illinois at Urbana-Champaign

Mardi Mahaffy, Humanities Librarian, New Mexico State University, Las Cruces, New Mexico

Sue Samson, Professor, Humanities Librarian, and Library Instruction Coordinator, The University of Montana, Missoula

Corey Seeman, Director, Kresge Business Administration Library, Ross School of Business, University of Michigan (Ann Arbor)

Roberta Stevens, 2010-2011 President of the American Library Association

Sue Stroyan, PhD, Information Services Librarian, Ames Library, Illinois Wesleyan University, Bloomington, Illinois

Heather Zabriskie, Youth Programs Coordinator, Orange County Library System, Orlando, Florida, 2010 Florida Library of the Year

PART I
The Manager Role

1

BEATING THE CLOCK: ADAPTIVE TIME MANAGEMENT IN A FLUID ENVIRONMENT

Geoffrey P. Timms

MANAGING OUR time would be easy if the environment in which we worked was stable, consistent, and predictable. This is not the reality in which most of us function. The unexpected regularly encroaches, threatening to hinder our plans and consume our time. We can prepare ourselves to master our schedules, even when we are not fully in control of what we must address.

DEVELOP A ROUTINE

At the beginning of the year we may each have goals and priorities in mind as well as a clear understanding of our daily responsibilities. An effective way to ensure that regular tasks are accomplished is to perform them in a routine, predictable way, perhaps even at the same time each day or week. Comprehensive tasks, associated with goals, can be allocated their own routines. We might set aside a partial day each week for a specific activity to ensure that over time we give it due attention. For goals that we must accomplish in a short time span, we may need to allocate priority time during a specific week to ensure their timely fulfillment. Sometimes I alert colleagues that my open-door policy is suspended (except for emergencies) during specific hours. Productivity software, such as Google Calendar, can be invaluable for organizing time each week. By using this visual tool, we can easily identify unallocated time and be reminded about specific tasks. With Google Calendar, multiple calendars can be viewed simultaneously.

QUICK TIP

Set aside regular time to read e-mail and deal with each message just once.

Many of us deal with endless streams of tasks, trickling steadily into our lives through e-mail. Taking time to read, process, and file e-mail is an essential part of staying on the ball. Strategies for managing e-mail and the tasks they bring us include these:

- If it should be deleted and forgotten, do so immediately.
- If it can be dealt with swiftly and now, get it done and delete the e-mail.
- Use a separate e-mail account for personal e-mail.
- Forward (delegate) tasks to those who should address them.
- Take time weekly to clear up the in-box.

- Develop a filing system and use it, making your old e-mail much easier to find.
- Take advantage of e-mail filtering to send messages from mailing lists directly to folders and focus on them at a specific time.
- Avoid double-handling any task.

MAINTAIN PERSPECTIVE

When unexpected tasks are added to our workload with little warning, we can be tempted to fall into the trap of feeling overwhelmed. We may indeed actually be overwhelmed, burdened with an impossible set of tasks to complete in a set time frame. Feeling overwhelmed, however, can lead to a reflective paralysis in which one focuses on the enormity of the combined tasks without actually making progress on anything. We can avoid this by maintaining perspective and by being prepared with a system for prioritizing tasks. Perspective recognizes that we can hold ourselves responsible to accomplish only so much in a given time frame. Prioritizing enables us to make the best choices about what we try to tackle and to focus on specific tasks.

QUICK TIP

Turn the negative energy of worry into the positive energy of action by focusing on one task rather than all of them.

For the perfectionist, it is difficult to say of a task, "That's good enough." Although we may have a desire to complete each task with a high level of quality, there are times when we need to accept that a task has been completed sufficiently and that it is time to move on to the next one. This is by no means negligence but more a recognition that a productivity/quality tradeoff exists. There is a time to emphasize quality, but there is also a time to focus on getting multiple tasks completed.

QUICK TIP

Improve your effectiveness by documenting and tackling tasks according to their priority. Look for opportunities to complete tasks according to available time.

DOCUMENT AND PRIORITIZE TASKS

Keeping a running list of tasks helps to focus the mind and avoid the time wasted when perspective is lost. There is no need to wonder what to tackle next when an up-to-date ranked list of tasks is at hand. I maintain two lists that sit prominently on my desk. One is my annual goals document, which contains a breakdown of the main tasks I must tackle. The other is a running list of the tasks that arise every day. The running list has two columns representing categories of priority and a third column for lesser tasks, each of which should require thirty minutes or less to complete. As each additional task arises, I add it to one of the three columns on the basis of its urgency. Within its column I rank it with a note or symbol to identify its priority within the list. Also included are tasks from the goals document. In this way, I always have a quick reference document at hand, and it is clear what I must address next.

Lists also help us fill unused time slots. After we have worked most of the morning on a task and have thirty minutes left before lunch, a list helps us identify tasks we can complete within that time. This helps us avoid wasting thirty minutes of the day in anticipation of lunch. Ideally we should complete tasks in one session, especially those that require deep concentration. For me, this is particularly true of trouble-shooting errors in computer scripts. I need sufficient time to immerse myself in the logic and language of scripts. I find it fruitless to spend fragmented time on such tasks; I achieve results much more effectively when addressing them in one sitting.

THINK BROADLY

With so many tasks and projects being collaborative or interdependent, it follows that the success of others may depend on us. When a colleague approaches me with a request for logistical support, it is tempting to prioritize it lower than the tasks for which I am directly responsible. That, however, would be shortsighted. Thinking more broadly about the library as a whole, I try to recognize that helping colleagues overcome hurdles frees them up to advance their own contributions toward the library's goals. This may have to be accomplished at the expense of parts of my own agenda for the week. As long as we honestly address both our and others' priorities with a broad perspective in mind and come to the conclusion that such a sacrifice is best for the overall efficiency of the library, we can consider it time well spent.

COMMUNICATE TIME ISSUES

It is widely agreed that of the 24 hours in a day we can work only so much before we drop. Similarly, good supervisors are aware and accepting of the need to readdress plans when the unexpected occurs. Arming ourselves with accurate information and identifying and agreeing on priorities eliminate much of the worry associated with being overwhelmed. It is also noteworthy that it is better to be up front and honest than to surprise a supervisor with the news that a task is incomplete. The impact can affect other colleagues if their work is dependent on our own. Finally, it is important to enjoy the satisfaction of completing a task. A quick walk around the library or a trip to the coffeepot can be considered time well invested if it helps refresh the mind and transition between tasks. The key is to not get tempted to go chat to a colleague for half an hour and spend the time unwisely.

QUICK TIP

Welcome opportunities to help others be effective in their tasks; interdependency is necessary for accomplishing common goals.

2
CREATING MANUALS FOR JOB DUTIES
Holly Flynn

THERE ARE many good reasons for a librarian to create a manual of his or her job duties. In the event that a librarian goes on a leave of absence—whether long-term or short-term—a manual provides management documentation for getting that librarian's assigned tasks completed in the interim. When a librarian retires, a manual is a way to pass on institutional knowledge that might not be documented elsewhere. Even if a manual is never used while a librarian is away, it helps the librarian writing it to become better organized, as I have experienced myself.

I have gone on two maternity leaves in three years, for a total of six months. During my first leave I was the solo librarian at two branch libraries and managed one full-time library assistant. For the second leave, I managed two full-time assistants at two locations, one sixty miles away from our main campus. I knew that, given the economy and poor budget years, a temporary librarian would not be hired to replace me. I needed to train several colleagues to fill in while I was gone. I also needed to ensure that my patrons were not inconvenienced during this time. Finally, I wanted my library assistants to refer inquiries to other librarians instead of acting as librarians and risk working above their union pay grade.

Writing a job manual is a bit like trying to write a parenting manual: it is going to be different for everyone, and you cannot possibly cover every contingency. There are, however, a few basic steps you can take to be successful: keep a log of your daily tasks; write down personal practices and procedures; find backups and train them; and record passwords and contact information.

KEEP TRACK OF EVERYTHING YOU DO

Most of us cram many tasks into a single workday: possibly a reference shift, a library instruction class, story time, committee meetings, and more. Try to keep a fairly detailed list of everything you work on for several weeks. As you read through it later, it will become clear what you spend the most time on and what your highest priorities are. This helps you later when you start writing down policies and procedures for these tasks. If you are a reference librarian, keep track of all the questions you are asked and where to find the answers. If your library uses a software program for keeping statistics, such as DeskTracker, you can notate your statistics there and run a report later.

WRITE DOWN PERSONAL PRACTICES AND PROCEDURES FOR EACH AREA OF YOUR JOB

If your library has general procedures in place and current documentation for them, there is no need to rewrite that. You may want to include reference to the relevant public web pages in your manual, since those are usually kept more up to date than private documentation. However, if you do something differently, or have different priorities than other librarians, write those down. Include every detail. Remember that, although you may do tasks much like others at your library, you probably have your own unique way of doing them. Think of the librarian who has worked at your library for thirty years or more. She knows her subject area and patrons thoroughly. Eventually she will retire, and without a written manual all of that knowledge will be lost. Manuals are an excellent way to preserve the institutional memory of an organization. Not only do they work as a stopgap for management until a new person is hired, they are also a valuable tool for the new librarian.

FIND SEVERAL PEOPLE TO FILL IN FOR YOU, AND TRAIN THEM

Once you have the main components of your manual—procedures for various areas of responsibility—you need to find colleagues to serve as your substitute in each area. In the event that you are unavailable to work for a while, this assures that each aspect of your job is covered while not overworking any one person. For instance, if you work the reference desk, have another reference librarian cover your reference questions, whether they are presented in person, through e-mail, or chat. If you are a subject selector, have another collections colleague with a similar subject area trained to buy books and other material for you in the event that your patrons request something. If you need someone with specialized expertise, you may want to work with someone from your professional organization. Generally speaking, if you know you are going to be gone only for a short time, others are usually willing to help.

When it comes to training your temporary stand-ins, simply giving them a copy of your manual is not enough. Work with them personally to ensure that they can handle the details of your job. Cross-training is an exercise that has only positive effects.

You may also create online tutorials for areas of your job for which you have no backup. If you are a subject librarian, you might create online instruction modules for various databases using software such as Adobe Acrobat Connect Pro. I created a virtual tour of our library for patrons to use, since I knew I would be unavailable for in-person tours at the beginning of the semester. Finally, make sure your public online documentation, such as research guides and collection development policies, is accurate and up to date.

RECORD RELEVANT PASSWORDS AND CONTACT INFORMATION

If your backups need to know various computer passwords or other numbers, include those in the manual. As I was preparing for a leave of absence, our security gates occasionally malfunctioned, so I included the phone number to call and the serial numbers of the gates in my manual. You can hide your manual in a password-protected wiki so only authorized people can see it. Also be sure to include the contact information for all of your backups as well as your home or cell phone number. Distribute the link and password to your manual to your supervisors, appropriate employees, and anyone else you think may need it. In the end, this will likely mean fewer phone calls to you at home, and you will be free to concentrate on nonwork issues. Finally, be sure to revisit your manual once a year to make sure it is up to date, in the event that you are unexpectedly called away from your job.

Creating a manual for my job duties has been extremely useful. My manual was used successfully during my two maternity leaves and continues to be used now that I am on an academic year appointment and out of the office for three months a year. The process of writing the manual helped me better organize my job procedures. By letting my colleagues handle various tasks, I am able to leave the office for extended periods and not be overwhelmed with outstanding work on my return. In a challenging economy when management may be unable to hire temporary librarians, manual documentation and cross-training are budget-friendly ways to handle long- or short-term leaves. Manual writing is also an excellent way to pass on best practices and institutional memory after you retire. Whether you are new to your career or ready to retire, having a manual for your library contributions will endear you to your colleagues and management.

3

HOW TO MANAGE SERVING STUDENTS OF GENERATIONAL POVERTY

Kris Baughman and Rebecca Marcum Parker

SERVING STUDENTS of generational poverty as a school librarian is rewarding as well as challenging, especially during a recession. In addition to giving students library and information technology skills, you can teach them many of the societal norms other students are already equipped with when they come to school. School and reading may not be a priority at home if paying the gas bill and keeping food on the table are daily concerns for parents.

BEHAVIOR MANAGEMENT

Students from a generational poverty background need clear expectations, examples of excellence, and consistent structure. At the beginning of each school year, and if your population is transient at the beginning of the second semester, review your expectations. Have them posted clearly in the library, and word them in a positive way. Be sure to follow them yourself. It is important to talk to students in the voice of an equal—many of them may be running households and raising siblings at home, and they are accustomed to having an adult role. Model expectations and praise students who exhibit positive behaviors. Explain that every place has rules, and that knowing those expectations is part of being successful. Create relationships with the students that show them you have an interest in them. This entices them to follow your lead. Use humor when possible—lessons and skills stick when laughter is part of the memory of learning them. Expect to have to teach and model even the most basic expectations. Teach students that they control what happens to them via good choices and otherwise. Here are examples of good expectations to post and use:

- *"Respect others."* Explain that we must treat others as we want to be treated. I always address the students as "ladies" and "gentlemen" to create the expectation that they will behave well.
- *"Listen carefully and follow the directions."* Explain that this means hearing and doing what you ask.
- *"Ask questions when you don't understand."* Be sure students know you are serious about this, because you need to find out if you should start a unit with more fundamental information.
- *"Take care of all library materials, furniture, and equipment."* Give specific examples and model what this looks like.
- *"Use a right-size, indoor voice."* Model this for the students; in many generational poverty homes volume equals power.

RELATIONSHIPS WITH PARENTS AND GUARDIANS

Adults in generational poverty situations are stretched in many different directions. During a recession, services and charitable funds are less available than in better times. Many parents may be working more than one job and may have limited time available to aid their children. Also, many adults in generational poverty did not have successful school careers and may be leery of talking to school staff. Consider these approaches and ideas:

- Help parents feel at ease. Gear your language choices to what will be easiest to understand, and listen carefully to responses in order to adjust, if necessary.
- If time permits, try to meet parents early in the year to establish the start of a positive relationship.
- Tell parents about your positive observations of their child first, especially if you have a concern.
- Use teamwork language, and reaffirm how much they have to offer in working with their child.
- If they feel that any particular challenge makes them less capable of helping their child, tell them of your own parenting challenges and concerns, if possible.

CHECKING OUT LIBRARY BOOKS

Generational poverty students may not have experienced the best library situations, since such students tend to be migratory and in environments that may not offer consistency. Consequently, these students may have had challenges in the past returning library books. The big lesson that helps students is learning to take responsibility for and communicating about mistakes.

- Have students and parents sign a library contract that covers book care and responsibility, including your library expectations. Write the contract using simple language in case a parent is challenged by reading. Offer translations, if necessary.
- Let students know that there is a solution to every problem. Tell them that situations resolve in a more positive way when they let you know about books lost during evictions, other transitions, or other problems. Do extensive role playing to show students how to communicate this way.
- Keep open lines of communications with classroom teachers so that you learn of challenges students are facing.
- Consider, if the budget permits, forgiving books lost due to circumstances beyond the student's control, such as an eviction, or allowing students to donate a book to "pay for" a lost book. Tell students that you will forgive the book loss on the condition that, if they ever get the book back, they will return it to the library.
- Allow students with lost books to check out additional books on a "payment plan." Any time a student with lost books wants to check a book out, ask that he or she pay at least fifty cents toward the lost book(s). If your budget allows, forgive the rest of the cost of the book at the end of the year if the student has made at least five payments, or a number you determine.
- Be willing to advocate at the public library for students with lost public library books, and offer public library book return services to students. Public libraries have become more flexible, and many forgive fines and work with families regarding lost books.

COLLECTION MANAGEMENT

Many libraries are underfunded, especially during a recession. In addition to the standard sources of funding, such as school moneys and book fair proceeds, consider these options:

- Shamelessly plead for donations of goods and services from merchants, especially bookstores. Widen your circle to include businesses outside of your school neighborhood or district; business persons in suburban areas often say they have not been approached by any school before. Most offer something and are happy to have the tax break from the donation. Anything you cannot use can be given to a classroom or offered as a student incentive.

- Ask how much businesses can donate instead asking if they will donate. Make them tell you no. Always be pleasant and appreciative.
- Try not to ever turn down a donation; if others are accustomed to you always accepting what they offer, they will think of offering to donate more often.
- If possible, buy from discount bookstores and garage sales. Ask for discounts or free items. I have often gone to garage sales in suburban areas where the sellers were happy to let a librarian or teacher collect items for free at the end of the sale.
- Constantly talk to family and friends about needs in your library. Ask them to connect you to others.
- Ask students to write letters asking for donations and thanking those who have donated. Establishing a personal connection with donors makes your needs tangible—they then have a child's face to attach to the beneficiaries of their donations.

Preparing our students for a happy, productive adulthood is labor intensive, and school librarianship during a recession is a challenge. Be open to unconventional solutions. These students' futures depend on your approach to managing your library effectively and creatively.

4

HOW TO PROTECT YOUR LIBRARY FROM EMPLOYMENT DISCRIMINATION CLAIMS

Michael A. Germano

THE COSTS of defending, settling, or paying damages for a verdict related to a claim of employment discrimination can be substantial for most organizations and potentially debilitating for a cash-strapped library. Money that goes toward compensating aggrieved employees can represent significant lost resources for patron services, the collection, and a library's physical plant or building. Even in the current economically challenging times, it makes more sense to put resources into discrimination and harassment prevention programs than into cutting corners here.[1] The expense of a prevention program including training workshops, updating policies and handbooks, as well as review by an attorney could easily be less than the charges associated with a single employment discrimination claim.

Where do such claims arise? Where are the danger areas for managers in terms of provoking a claim of discrimination? An employee can allege that discrimination took place in a wide number of scenarios. Common ones include these:

- hiring and interviewing
- termination of employment including layoffs
- performance evaluations
- promotions
- demotions
- leaves for family care
- disability leaves
- changes in benefits
- performance management
- changes in work hours
- changes in work assignment

Each of these areas represents potentially highly risky behaviors on the part of managers. For example, faulty language in a job description or recruitment posting could create problems related to discrimination in hiring. Interviewers risk asking illegal questions such as inquiry into an applicant's health status or pregnancy or the exact nature of a disability that would have absolutely no bearing on the ability to perform a job. By the same token, changes in work hours and work assignment, if not conducted equitably and neutrally according to a policy that is nondiscriminatory, could pose significant problems as well.

The best way to prevent accusations of discriminatory behavior arising from managerial actions is an ongoing, preemptive strategy that ensures that all library policies and procedures are up to date and compliant with current federal, state, and local employment discrimination laws.[2] Additionally, established library proce-

---

DOES "FAIR" ALWAYS MEAN TREATING EVERYONE THE SAME?

Absolutely not. Managers who equate fairness with treating everyone the same are missing the point. Sometimes the law requires managers to treat employees differently. Most disability law is based on this concept in the form of "reasonable accommodation." For many managers it becomes trickier when the issue is one of perceived favoritism or when the opposite is true in the form of employee discipline. As long as the favoritism or disciplinary action is not based on a protected characteristic, it is legal and can indeed be a great tool for motivating employees or managing performance.

MANAGER HANDBOOKS

Everyone is aware of the concept of an employee handbook, but what about a manager handbook? Not as widely used, manager handbooks can represent a codification of policies, behaviors, and appropriate actions required by managers. For example, a manager handbook could detail the scope and limits of performance reviews to ensure that they are compliant with applicable labor and employment laws. Another suggested use of manager handbooks is a process and set of rules for documenting all employee actions in accordance with stated policies and retaining that documentation in an organized way. Manager handbooks are a relatively new concept but could represent an enormous benefit in terms of managing risk related to managerial actions and behaviors.

dures should ensure accurate record keeping and documentation on the part of the library's managers that reflect adherence to those policies. Specifically, your library should follow these guidelines:

- Review and update all job descriptions including the language used in postings to ensure that there is nothing amiss or problematic in terms of discrimination, especially with regard to disabilities.
- Provide training for employees and managers alike on harassment and disability compliance particularly.
- Make sure performance evaluation processes are updated and standardized on the basis of objective criteria.
- Update benefits and leave policies, especially those related to family leave, disability leaves, and military deployment as well as terminations and benefit continuance requirements.
- Create or update employee and manager handbooks that reflect policies that are clear in their intolerance of discrimination or harassment by all workers.
- Establish a clear disciplinary procedure, marked by progressive warnings for poor performance or unacceptable conduct, that requires consistent documentation and record keeping.
- Ensure ongoing training, especially as the law evolves and includes new protections against potential forms of discrimination.
- Always keep abreast of state and local laws, which often are more progressive and inclusive in terms of offering protections.

Training is particularly valuable in terms of heading off claims of harassment, of any kind, which can often lead to a discrimination complaint. Investing in training for employees and managers can be money well spent, even in times of budgetary pressures, since the cost of training programs, especially web-based ones, is a fraction of the cost associated with a single discrimination claim.[3]

With that said, for all of the above tactics to succeed there needs to be a firm understanding by managers that their activities can always lead to accusations, even groundless ones, and as a result must be documented conscientiously and scrupulously. For example, if there is a documented policy outlining the steps a manager must go through to discipline substandard performance that features objective criteria of performance, fair evaluations, and escalating warnings, all of those protective measures are in vain if no documentation exists to validate that the nondiscriminatory process was followed. Managers need to be trained not only to identify high-risk areas like interviewing, performance evaluations, and performance management but also to document their decisions and actions effectively and accurately to demonstrate how they followed policies on the basis of fairness and equal opportunity.[4]

Employment discrimination claims arise when there is action, or even the perception of action, by managers directed at an employee because of a protected characteristic like race, gender, age, national origin, religious affiliation, disability, or, increasingly, sexual orientation. Simply put, none of these characteristics can be relevant to a manager's decision about hiring, firing, promotion, demotion, job assignment, leaves, performance evaluations, or employee discipline or performance management. Creating policies and taking the time to educate managers and employees alike on those policies along with the processes for following them is a critical first step to avoiding discrimination claims. Additionally helpful is creating an environment where diversity is embraced by all employees, including managers, by offering ongoing training related to diversity-based laws and policies. Finally, focusing on training and resources for managers so that they stay up to date and are well versed in policies related to managerial actions and their impact on protected characteristics, as well as the requirements for documenting those actions, is a crucial last step. Following these steps goes a long way toward ensuring that your library is not on the receiving end of a discrimination claim or lawsuit.

Notes

1. Lynn D. Lieber, "Why Training Dollars Should Remain in HR's Recession Budgets," *Employment Relations Today* 36 (Fall 2009): 115–20.
2. "Take a Policy Approach to Fight Discrimination Claims," *HR Focus* 86, no. 8 (2009): 1–15.
3. "How to Use Training to Bulletproof Your Firm against Suits," *Law Office Management and Administration Report* 6, no. 9 (2006): 1–15.
4. Cedric Herring, "Does Diversity Pay? Race, Gender, and the Business Case for Diversity," *American Sociological Review* 74, no. 2 (2009): 208–24.

5

MANAGING EMERGENCIES: WHAT TO DO WHEN BASIC OR BIG DISASTERS STRIKE

Sian Brannon and Kimberly Wells

PERHAPS YOU will never need any of the information provided here, but let's face it—chances are something unexpected is going to happen at your library. Emergencies can be large-scale disasters or they can be quickly developing situations. For all stages of emergencies, there are considerations for your building, including materials and processes that staff should be aware of for smooth handling of these situations. Create these contingency responses now, and hope you never have to use them.

GENERAL EMERGENCY SUPPLIES

An emergency supply tub contains initial supplies to be used during and after an emergency. (These are not the same as disaster-recovery supplies, which include materials to be used in the preservation efforts of damaged materials.) Every location should have at least one supply tub, containing supplies to be used during and after an emergency in their building. All levels of staff should know its location, and its contents should be reviewed periodically. One person needs to be responsible for keeping it stocked and checking expiration dates.

All of the supplies can be purchased at a home improvement store. Remember that, even though we sometimes have advance warning an emergency (freezes, wildfires, etc.), these are the items that will fly off the shelves as your community prepares for the worst. Staff time should not be wasted trying to track these items down, so buy them ahead of time. The purpose of having general emergency supplies on hand is usually for the most basic types of emergencies, such as a leak in the roof, a power outage, first-aid needs, or a small fire. Make sure you have these items in your emergency supply tub:

- ❏ copy of current emergency manual
- ❏ first-aid kit
- ❏ gloves—rubber gloves and work gloves, at least two pair
- ❏ plastic sheeting—can be used to drape stacks to fend off moisture
- ❏ towels
- ❏ garbage bags
- ❏ duct tape
- ❏ flashlights

❑ batteries—with the expiration date written in large numbers on the package
❑ pens/markers
❑ scissors
❑ caution tape—in case you need to barricade a certain area of the library
❑ incident report forms—blank forms that can be filled out quickly, as soon as possible after an emergency so nothing is forgotten
❑ clipboard
❑ phone numbers for local emergency services
❑ fire extinguisher, kitchen-size—and be sure to keep track of its expiration date
❑ maps of building and evacuation plan

DISASTER RECOVERY

Sometimes emergencies are much bigger. After a tornado, flood, or car coming through the front door, you have a lot of decisions to make, and when the dust settles you have to know what to do first. Begin by implementing your disaster recovery plan to determine which services to get back up and running. Include input from other departments, such as facilities and technology services, when you create your plan so that you have reasonable expectations and those departments are aware of your intentions after an emergency. Paper copies of these documents should stay in the trunk of your and your staff's car, because after a large emergency you are unlikely to be able to pull up an electronic copy on a staff computer.

A disaster team should be formed in advance. It should include the director, branch managers, librarians, and representative staff members who have the ability to assess the extent of damage to their collections, assign priorities, and make value judgments about salvaging and discarding. Each member of the team should keep a copy of the disaster plan at home. Responsibilities of the disaster team are as follows:

- Assign a member of the team to keep a written account of the disaster and recovery process by maintaining a log of activities arranged chronologically by date and time.
- Establish a command post at the disaster site, complete with desk, office supplies, and access to a phone. The library's insurance company should offer assistance and provide phones, electricity, and so forth.
- Assess damage and gather appropriate equipment and supplies to begin recovery efforts.
- Oversee the stabilization of the disaster area and help direct and record the removal of damaged materials.

There are other people to keep in mind when you are dealing with disaster recovery. You may need phone numbers and contacts for cold-storage or freeze-drying businesses, pallet companies, refrigerated trucking, and companies from which to order dehumidifiers, generators, wet-dry vacuums, water pumps, and fans.

A comprehensive disaster recovery plan should include the following:

- *List of personnel to notify immediately.* This should include the emergency contact information for your director, principal, dean, or city manager, technology coordinator, and facilities caretakers.
- *List of priorities for saving collections.* Should fire fighters rescue the children's materials first, or a special collection of local history donated by town elders? These decisions should be made ahead of time and not in the chaos of recovery.
- *List of staff responsibilities.* Assign collections and records to specific staff so they can oversee removal and salvage of those collections.
- *Recovery process.* Include basic salvage instructions.
- *List of supplies and vendors.* You might need a wet-dry vacuum, walkie-talkies, or portable drying fans. Make a list of such items and the departments or businesses that can provide them. Even if they are items that are commonly provided by your facilities department, they may be assigned to areas with higher priority in the city, so this can be very helpful.
- *Instructions.* Here is where details come in. Consult with preservation department staff or your library cooperative to determine and list procedures for salvaging items damaged by water or fire.
- *Safety information.* Do not forget to include safety information regarding drills, use of emergency equipment, and advice regarding health issues such as mold.

BASIC RECOVERY RULES

- Do not open or close wet books.
- Do not separate single sheets.
- Do not remove book covers.
- Do not wring or press wet books or papers.
- Do not wipe off mud and dirt.
- Do not stack books.
- Do not unpack wet file boxes containing papers, prints, drawings, microfilm, or photographs.

GENERAL SAFETY MEASURES

Check the following on an annual basis:

- ❏ air conditioning
- ❏ alarm system
- ❏ batteries for alarm system (clean corrosion, etc.)
- ❏ emergency lighting
- ❏ fire extinguishers
- ❏ flashlights and batteries
- ❏ heating system
- ❏ insurance coverage
- ❏ pipes for leaks
- ❏ plumbing
- ❏ smoke alarm system
- ❏ transistor radios and batteries
- ❏ water detectors

Make location maps that indicate where all in-house emergency equipment is kept, and post these in each department. Post emergency phone numbers in each department. Make sure that each area has a fire extinguisher as well as a transistor radio and flashlight.

Make sure that computer storage is updated regularly and kept in a safe place.

Have regular fire, tornado, and other disaster drills.

None of these things will have any impact if your staff does not know the locations of your manuals or supply tubs, or if they are not trained to use their contents. The number-one goal during a crisis is keeping your staff and customers safe, and these supplies and manuals will go a long way in helping accomplish that goal.

6

CREATING A STAFF ACCOUNTABILITY SYSTEM

Terry Ann Lawler

YOU CANNOT afford to take any employee for granted. Nor can you afford to ignore lagging performance. Good managers know that they must take the blame when things are not going well. But how do they find a way to make everything go right? Creating an accountability system that is fair and simply implemented is not difficult. You *can* hold staff accountable for performance. Starting a new system can be frightening to staff who are used to the status quo. You can overcome fear and achieve staff buy-in with your system by asking them for input on the process and detailing your end results (more items shelved, happier customers, etc.). Consider the plan outlined below, or create your own design based on these ideas.

First, you must identify the primary issues among your staff. Observe, observe, observe. Are they always behind schedule with regular tasks? If so, why? Is it one individual? A group problem? Once you have pinpointed a few key areas, contact your human resources department and find out what the official policies are, if any, regarding the problems you have identified. For example, your library may have strict guidelines regarding use of phones or e-mail on staff time. In this case, rules would just need enforcing, not creating. Sometimes it is easier to pinpoint exactly where team difficulties lie by interviewing coworkers and colleagues who are not on your staff but see them on a regular basis.

Next, continue with an informal but mandatory staff meeting. The sole purpose of this meeting is to set expectations. Focus on just a few key topics. During the session, ask your staff for their input regarding new ground rules. Be sure to take into consideration anything they add that may help. Give everyone a voice regarding improvement. The staff may have good ideas for consequences or self-regulation. By using their suggestions, you achieve a win-win agreement and staff buy-in. Staff are more likely to adhere to rules that they help develop.

Also during the meeting, set specific team goals. Clearly defined goals are a must. Tell your employees what you want from them. For example, you may be telling them that you will not tolerate gossip. You would explain that gossip is detrimental to staff morale, lowers productivity, hurts people, and is against the rules. Tell your staff that, if they wish to complain about another staff member, they need to do it with you, in private. Then explain the consequences of gossiping, using your library's official discipline policy. Make sure that everyone has a clear understanding of the rules and consequences. If you do not have the time to gather all of your staff at once, do a series of mini-meetings each covering the same content. Assemble questions that are asked during each meeting and post them with answers in your staff area. Finally, document the meeting. Take notes and save them so that you can refer to them later, during individual employee discussions if the need arises.

Once you have laid out the ground rules, your staff should all be clear about what is expected from them. Implement your regulations immediately after the meeting. Remain impartial. Employees should understand that you reward compliance and enforce policies without exception. Then, give your staff a chance to succeed. Remember to reward good behavior immediately.

Use an "open door" policy to ensure that complaints go directly to you. Make it clear that your staff can approach you about issues confidentially and without repercussion. Some staff may feel more comfortable talking to you alone rather than bringing up issues in front of a group. Remain encouraging, positive, and supportive and use active listening when you do get complaints. If you do not know the answer to something, it is acceptable to say, "I don't know, but I'll find out." Remember to get back to your staff as soon as possible with that answer. If you are busy, remember that it is usually reasonable to ask to meet an employee at another date when you will have more time to talk.

THINGS TO REMEMBER
Never leave anyone on the bench.

Distribute a questionnaire. Ask staff to describe each task they do and what is involved from preparation to completion. This information helps you to identify which tasks employees are completing and how they assign primacy. You may find that a prioritization is required and can solve many issues. Develop a list of each employee's daily, weekly, and monthly tasks in order to gauge how evenly the work load is spread. Reassign tasks if necessary.

Next, use the task list you have assembled from the questionnaire to do a time study. Make a list of all team responsibilities. A simple Excel chart works fine. Have a column for starting and ending times, number of items handled, number of customers assisted, number of carts shelved, or whatever other measure is appropriate. Give one to each staff member. For one week staff should record starting times and ending times, how many items they handled, and any useful comments.

THINGS TO REMEMBER
Keep your ground rules simple.

Using the time study, come up with average acceptable times for each assignment. Make a list of duties and the time it should take to do each. Post these times in the staff work area.

Hold a short meeting to discuss the new criteria. Ask staff for input and make applicable changes. Implement the standards with the use of a daily schedule. Hold staff accountable to their scheduled items. Speak with staff who are not following the schedule and find out why. You can assign the creation of the daily schedule to a senior staff member, but monitor it for fairness.

Yes, there will be paperwork. You will need to begin recording data and figuring statistics. Create a daily notebook for your staff, or have them turn in slips with finished tasks to you after each shift. Make it an expectation that your employees record how many carts they are shelving, reports they are running, and the like. Team members should be aware of their own performance levels and should not be surprised if you need to speak with them. You can post statistics in bar graph form in the staff work area. This makes it easy to reward your highest achievers and immediately redirect your lowest.

An important part of good management is giving credit to your employees when things go right. Rewarding regularly is an essential part of accountability. Employees work harder and better when they know they are appreciated. Be creative. You can have a grab bag of goodies, a kudos wall, or employee of the month awards. You are limited only by your own imagination.

Having accountable employees is a factor in your own achievement. Hoping your employees figure out what they need to do on their own sets them and you up for failure. You help them attain success by setting expectations, implementing your agreements, providing feedback, enforcing standards, and rewarding progress. Using a systematic and consistent method gets your employees into compliance and accomplishes accountability.

7

PLANNING AHEAD:
TIME MANAGEMENT IN DEFINING GOALS

Geoffrey P. Timms

IN CURRENT library management, people and activities are typically focused on defining and fulfilling goals in accordance with the library's mission. Goals are usually defined collaboratively and specify how departments and individuals will function to achieve them. At any one time, a librarian may be contributing to multiple goals. It follows, then, that time management is a critical element in preparing to tackle the goals of the institution and to bring them to fruition in an appropriate time frame. This chapter offers ways to think in terms of time management as you define the library's goals.

IDENTIFY REQUIRED TASKS AND SKILL SETS

In we are defining goals, the planning of time allocation must account for the various skill sets needed to accomplish it. For example, the goal of subscribing to a new e-book collection and integrating it into the library catalog may require the participation of several individuals across several departments. To assess the potential time contribution of each person, we must scrutinize the tasks required to accomplish the goal. For example,

- The electronic resources librarian must negotiate and sign a license agreement.
- The cataloger must customize the MARC records and upload them into the library catalog.
- The systems librarian must configure the proxy server to permit remote access.
- The subject librarians and web master must publicize the new e-book collection.

Ongoing tasks might include regularly adding and deleting MARC records as the e-book collection changes over time; monitoring web server logs due to the additional information captured each time an e-book is accessed from the catalog; and gathering and processing e-book usage data.

This is an example of a relatively concise goal, yet with a little thought we have identified several tasks and skills required of several people to bring about its completion and ongoing maintenance. This enables us to become more effective in managing and coordinating the time spent on each of these tasks. If a new skill set must be acquired to accomplish the goal, a realistic estimate of the time burden of learning and applying the skills must be calculated.

ESTABLISH PRIORITIES

The definition of goals is determined by the institutional mission, but the allocation of time and resources to their fulfillment is determined by priorities. Priorities are often ranked according to the institutional level from which they were conceived; for example, the priorities of the institutional administration and senior management are likely to be given high priority at the department level. Priority is also usually allocated to activities to which individuals assign high importance or urgency. However priorities are defined, they weigh heavily in the allocation of time devoted to specific activities.

Having identified the tasks required to accomplish the goal and each individual's anticipated contribution, we must consider the workload of the participating individuals and their priorities relative to the goal at hand. Priorities must be successfully negotiated before time commitments are made by participating individuals. This is where perspectives can complicate things. Colleagues may assign differing priorities to a particular activity according to their knowledge, perspectives, and specific function within the organization. For example, in a systems role I assign highest priority to ensuring system security and stability rather than to assisting with individual projects hosted on the system. Both are important, but one depends on the

QUICK TIP

Reduce a goal to its component tasks and identify the people and skills needed to complete it.

other, so the priority is clear. Time management at this stage, therefore, requires that we practice the skills of diplomacy, negotiation, and effective communication with colleagues.

UNDERSTAND PERSONAL PRODUCTION CAPACITY

As each of us weighs the potential time commitments we would contribute to the goals in question, we must consider our personal production capacity. It is easy to agree to partici-pate in many activities without contemplating the aggregate workload and regret it later. Whether we are aware of it or

not, each of us has a typical pace at which we accomplish specific types of activities. Some of us dwell on details and refinements; others complete tasks to their satisfac-tion on the first attempt. Some of us are more adept at specific tasks than others, each to our own skill set. It is important that we become aware of the time it takes us to accomplish the tasks in question or at least tasks similar in nature. Strategies to synthesize this information include listing the time commitments required to fulfill the day-to-day necessities of the job; listing the estimated time burden of additional activities that new goals would bring; ranking tasks by priority, which adds another useful dimension to the information listed; and utilizing human resources documents in which time allocated to routine tasks is formally declared for specific positions.

By maintaining a time allocation document, we can become much clearer about whether we are in danger of overextending ourselves or our subordinates beyond what is sustainable over time. Although people can work in overdrive for a time, nobody should be expected (or demand of themselves) to do so indefinitely. The result can be reduced morale and burnout, which reduce productivity overall.

PLAN FOR PROGRESS

Another reality about allocating time and resources to specific activities is that effec-tive management usually expects an accounting of both the inputs (money, time, tangible resources) and the resulting benefits (both to the library and its patrons). It is important to contemplate and justify the time invested in any given activity so that, at the goal's completion or at a predetermined evaluation point, the productivity of each of the inputs, time included, can be assessed. To keep track of this over time, when a goal is being agreed upon create a spreadsheet that outlines the specific tasks to be undertaken. It is prudent to assign a date by which each task must be completed, because this helps to maintain focus and momentum. Additionally, including a time log enables the documentation of time contributions to specific tasks. The value of this information is that it builds knowledge about personal and departmental pro-duction capacity and helps with considerations of time commitments when we set goals in the future.

It can be tempting to neglect planning time contributions for future activities and adopt a "we'll get it done" attitude. But when we devote time to thinking through the implications and consequences of undertaking a project, we gain an awareness of the opportunity cost (the cost of the alternative foregone). Rarely in the current economic climate do we tolerate or enjoy excess capacity in our libraries, so most new endeavors are undertaken at the expense of something else. It is, therefore, our responsibility to make ourselves fully aware of the priorities and production capacities that exist for ourselves and for our libraries and to allocate our time accordingly. By proactively managing time during goal setting, we can improve our efficiency and enhance our ability to use this valuable resource wisely.

8

TRANSFORMING AN OFF-CAMPUS LIBRARY FROM EMPTY SPACE TO AWARD WINNER IN ONE YEAR

Seamus Scanlon

WITHIN A year of the appointment of a full-time librarian at a satellite campus of City College in New York City (CUNY), the library services offered by college's Center for Worker Education (CWE) earned a prestigious I Love My Librarian Award sponsored by the Carnegie Corporation of New York and the *New York Times* and administered by the American Library Association.[1] The library went from empty space to award-winning space in one year.

CWE caters to 750 nontraditional students (age 25 and up) comprising full-time workers, homemakers, retirees, and others with interrupted school attendance.[2] Classes are primarily run in the evenings and Saturdays to facilitate their schedules. A liberal agenda in the 1970s prompted New York City unions to establish CWE so their members could secure a college education. It later came under the jurisdiction of CUNY and currently offers a BA in interdisciplinary studies, a BS in early childhood education, and an MA in the studies of the Americas.

One disadvantage of any satellite library is a low profile because it is removed from the power center of the main campus. The corollary, however, can be a major advantage, because once outside the confines of the main campus you control the direction and management of the library service and develop an ambience that supports a student-centric library. The I Love My Librarian Award acknowledges library innovation and service, goals for which "being in charge" provides one with an innate advantage.

Another advantage in this case was the CUNY ethos and mission: "access and excellence." CUNY is known for educating many generations of immigrants (including nine Nobel laureates and nine Pulitzer prize winners to date), so the markers for excellence are there.

STAFFING CHALLENGES AT THE CWE LIBRARY

The absence of a full-time librarian at CWE had resulted in inconsistent service coverage, including absence of coverage late nights and Saturdays. It was difficult for a multitude of part-time librarians "bussed" from the main campus to build rapport with students and faculty, to provide individualized training in library skills, or to be proactive in promoting the library and its resources.

As a full-timer, I was able to serve on the information technology and scholarship committees, which built goodwill that resulted in positive support for subsequent requests for funding. I was also able to arrange training of faculty/staff in library skills, including one-on-one sessions, which highlighted the value and extent of our digital and other resources.

Overall, I adopted the prevailing ethos at CWE—intensively student-centric—and built on it through the library. As a result, I integrated quickly into the CWE culture and working life. I was able to demonstrate the efficacy of a professional library service for faculty (as well as students), which resulted in backing from the chair and dean when I requested resources.

INFORMATION TECHNOLOGY CHALLENGES AT THE CWE LIBRARY
Database Access

Initially, there was no smooth access to electronic resources because the IP address range at CWE was treated as off-campus. This was a major disincentive for any of our neophyte nontraditional students struggling with classes, schoolwork, or research papers. I was well positioned to attack this problem in several ways:

- highlighting the waste of resources—millions of dollars invested in scholarly articles and journals, but access thwarted
- advocating on behalf of our students, who had enough challenges without this one, which hindered their ability to research effectively and use the library with confidence
- recording how library workshops became moribund as students struggled to register for off-campus access during class and how barcodes (needed for off-campus) were often missing or invalid

- pursuing the problem vigorously with the computer services department to get answers and solutions

After I delineated the scope of the problem and outlining to dean and chair how these conditions hindered the learning process for our students and faculty, the dean brought pressure to the main campus. The three-year problem was resolved within three weeks. Now instruction classes are seamless. CWE feels like a satellite campus, and students, faculty, and staff more content.

Printers

Another information technology problem was our printers, with constant paper jams and print jobs hanging, resulting in bottlenecks in the library, queuing. and frustration. To address this set of problems, I

- recorded every instance of printer failure
- estimated and logged the amount of time taken to resolve each printer failure
- highlighted the frustration of students with full-time family and work loads who could not print simple assignments
- noted the poor return for students from the technology fee

In response, the dean authorized new printers and software upgrades for the following semester. After implementation, there were no further problems.

PCs and Software

Sluggish PCs in the library and outdated software hindered students from completing assignments and cast our efficacy as a library service in a poor light. I exposed the problem from several directions:

- recorded on spreadsheet the details of PCs—age, RAM, obvious anomalies
- compared the specifications of PCs at the library to those on the main campus
- highlighted the significant contrast between the inferior library PCs and the CWE computer lab PCs, which was putting library users at a disadvantage
- showed that our main-campus students were using later releases of software than students at CWE, poorly reflecting the CWE goal of "access and excellence"

As a result, the dean authorized new PCs and software upgrades. As chair of the technology committee, I was able to make it policy to be in the vanguard of installing software releases rather than trailing the constituent colleges.

Access to 500,000 Books

There was no access for CWE students to CUNY's 500,000 books via the intra-CUNY campus lending service. A modern academic library service needs access to books as well as electronic journals. The dearth of books at CWE made the absence of this service acute. I elaborated the problem in several ways:

- researched with the library system vendor and central CUNY library services how the lending service could be used by a satellite campus (rather than by a constituent college)
- highlighted to the dean the lack of books in the CWE library
- argued that at full capacity we would only ever have small numbers of books
- presented costing of service in terms of benefit to our students and value for money

Ultimately, the dean authorized a monthly fee so that the limited CWE holdings were augmented by 500,000 books held by the CUNY Libraries.

A variety of conditions and actions made the Center for Worker Education at the City College of New York a success. Autonomy of our library and strong support locally and at the main campus were essential. With the addition of a persistent full-time librarian capable of identifying information technology obstacles and recommending solutions for them in collaboration with computer services and technical support, consistent library service and staffing—and ultimately excellent service—became possible.

Notes

1. For more on the Love My Librarian Awards, see www.ilovelibraries.org/lovemylibrarian/09winners.cfm#scanlon.
2. The Center for Worker Education website: www1.ccny.cuny.edu/prospective/cwe.

9

WHEN YOU'RE NOT (EXACTLY) THE BOSS: HOW TO MANAGE EFFECTIVELY IN A "COORDINATOR" ROLE

Kim Becnel

IN MANY cases, library hierarchies are less than cut and dried. Managers who hold titles such as children's services coordinator or reference services coordinator can have ambiguous relationships with those staff members who work in their departments but are ultimately under the direct supervision of a branch manager. These ambiguous relationships can lead to unnecessary conflicts and divided loyalties, but the coordinator or department head role can be a rewarding and productive one if some basic principles and strategies are kept in mind. Developing a strong sense of teamwork in your department, maintaining a strong relationship with your employees' supervisors, and keeping your own role in perspective will help you make the most of your position in the library.

Develop a sense of teamwork and loyalty among all of your employees, no matter where they work. This sense of teamwork is important for morale, but it can also be crucial to your success as a coordinator. When you lack the power to reward or punish employees directly, you have to get their buy-in, make them feel like they are part of a team that is doing worthy work. If you can succeed at this, your staff members will do what you ask. The following strategies help keep your staff members from feeling isolated and remind them that they are part of a department with common goals and shared challenges:

- Get your staff together as often as you can for meetings and training sessions. These gatherings provide everyone on your team with a shared sense of purpose and reaffirm your common mission.
- At meetings, work with your team to set department goals and priorities. Do not only solicit their input. Use it.
- Try to visit your staff at their locations on a regular basis. It is vitally important that they feel like you are aware of and invested in what they are doing on a daily basis.
- Especially when budgets are tight and staffing is short, it can be hard to have meetings or trainings in which your entire staff is assembled. Create a forum for discussion such as an electronic message board open to all members of your department, full-time and part-time. Encourage staff to share ideas and post questions for discussion.

- Have staff from various branches work together in committees on system-wide projects so that they get used to depending on each other and sharing ideas.
- Create databases of successful program plans, bookmarks, and bibliographies so that staff members can easily share ideas and work products.
- Whenever possible, give staff the opportunity to travel together to workshops and training opportunities outside of your library system.

Create and maintain constructive relationships with your staff's direct supervisors. Keeping an ongoing and constructive dialog with branch managers enables you to manage your department in a way that works with, and not counter to, each branch's unique situation and needs. The suggestions below are great ways to collaborate with your staff's supervisors:

- Attend staff meetings that involve your team at all locations when possible. Not invited? Ask if you can sit in.
- Keep supervisors informed of training topics you cover and projects you have asked your staff to work on. Solicit their input on future training topics and projects that they feel would be especially helpful for their staff members.
- Solicit input from branch managers concerning the best days and times to hold meetings and trainings.
- Always remind your staff to double-check with their supervisors before confirming their attendance at a meeting or training you have scheduled.
- If you are not already doing so, offer to participate in the goal-setting and evaluative portions of the annual employee performance appraisal of each employee in your department.
- Even if you are unable to participate in the formal evaluation process, you can still observe and evaluate members of your department. Observe your staff in action and write up your observations to share with the staff member and his or her direct supervisor. For example, if you work as head of children's services, make an effort to regularly observe your staff members conducting programming and interacting with children in their departments. Writing up observations that offer praise and helpful suggestions for your staff members and providing this information to both staff members and their supervisor are a helpful way to share your expertise in your subject area.

Get some perspective on your own position. If you think of yourself as occupying a support role for your staff out at the branches, they will understand that your main goal is to help them do their jobs better. As a result, they will be much likelier to comply with your requests and do their best to meet goals you set. Try keeping the following tips in mind:

- Encourage your staff members to let you know how you can help them do their jobs better. Ask them to let you know what they need—supplies, training, books on certain subjects, advice—and then do your best to fill these needs in a timely manner.

- Make an effort to go out and assist your staff with a big event or on a particularly busy day. You will get a better sense of how they are performing and what they might need from you to improve their work, and, just as important, they will feel your commitment to them and their endeavors.

- Know that compromise may be necessary due to the specific environments that each staff member is working in. Make sure that you are aware of the specific conditions of each branch through visits and supervisor and staff input. Be willing to modify your goals and expectations for members of your team because of differences in their working environments. This can be especially important when planning systemwide events, such as the summer reading program. If you want to make your program consistent across all branches, you need to make sure you create something that is doable at all locations—what works in theory may not work everywhere in practice. Be prepared to change your program to one that will work everywhere or to allow your staff in various locations to make modifications necessary to make the program work in their environments.

The keys to success in a coordinator or department head role, then, are maintaining perspective and clear lines of communication. You, your staff, and the folks who directly supervise them ultimately share the same goal: providing the best library service to your community. To make that happen, you need to be sure that no one is working in isolation. Keep all lines of communication open and use them often. Work with your staff and branch managers to determine the goals of your department and the best ways to meet them at each location. Be willing to listen and to compromise, to serve as well as to lead, and your efforts will result in a more rewarding library experience for you, your employees, and your patrons.

10

COMMUNICATION AND STAFF AWARENESS IN THE BRANCH LIBRARY

Jason Kuhl

IF YOU have managed a library branch, you have been presented with challenges not faced by other library managers. How do you make sure your staff feel like part of the organization? How do you keep them aware and committed to the library's values? Mastering techniques for nurturing staff awareness and employing good communication skills go a long way toward helping you meet these challenges in any type of library.

WHAT'S SO DIFFERENT ABOUT BRANCH MANAGEMENT, ANYWAY?

Although every library is different, library branches tend to

- be located in residential areas and maintain more of a "neighborhood" feel than their centrally located counterparts
- employ staff that live in the neighborhood
- employ a greater percentage of paraprofessional staff
- not house any support departments or library administration
- have a relatively flat organizational structure with many job titles directly reporting to one person

STAFF AWARENESS

Keeping staff aware of the library's philosophy is one of a branch manager's greatest challenges. At a single-location library, staff may see the library director and other decision makers on a daily basis; this is not true at a branch. How can staff be kept aware of the library's values and mission when they rarely see its leadership?

The good news is that, as the branch manager, you have control of this situation. Make no mistake; it is your responsibility to see that your staff understand the organization's philosophy and the reasons behind it. Some directors are more involved with communicating their vision to frontline staff than others; regardless, the ultimate responsibility lies with you. Keep these ideas in mind:

- Professional reading is not just for professionals. Understand that your staff probably do not read professional journals or blogs; you may be surprised to find out what they do not know about the library world (see It's Up to You).

Compile a binder of interesting articles and give staff time to read them. Discuss at meetings.

- Make minutes of library board meetings available and see that staff review them.
- Send staff to professional development workshops or webinars. Do not assume that paraprofessional staff should attend workshops for nonprofessionals only. Require attendees to distribute materials and share what they learn. Be sure to issue reports from all of the workshops and conferences you attend, too.
- Be transparent. Unless instructed otherwise, share reports from library meetings, committees, and workgroups with your staff.
- Get your staff involved. Cross-train and rotate duties. Think about giving staff full responsibility for a project from planning and budgeting to implementation and assessment. The more you can increase the breadth of their experience, the more apt they are to become aware and involved.

COMMUNICATING BY E-MAIL

Good communication is critical for effective management. It is surprising how many managers do not think about the way they communicate with their staff. Reign in your e-mail. Since it is fast and convenient for the sender, it has become the instinctive way to communicate, but it is far from perfect, for several reasons:

- It is not immediate; if something is of critical importance, your busy staff may not see it until it is too late.
- It is best for one-way communications; even if one recipient responds, others do not have the benefit of the discussion unless all replies are sent to all recipients.
- It is asynchronous; if you send an e-mail to all of your staff, some will surely hear about it through the grapevine before they read it.

IT'S UP TO YOU . . .

. . . to make sure your staff are aware of major topics in the field. I recently spoke with some branch library paraprofessionals who thought their library was horribly mismanaged because they were under a hiring freeze and would not be getting raises that year. A glance at any professional journal would have shown them that innumerable libraries across the country are facing those very circumstances—and much worse—during these difficult times. Do not assume that staff members are aware of even the most important issues.

- It is overwhelming; the sheer volume of e-mail we receive each day can lead to overload and critical information being missed.

How many times have you said something like "It was in an e-mail. Didn't you read it?" to one of your staff who missed a key piece of information? E-mail is quick and easy; it is natural to want to use it whenever you have something to share. But instead of overloading your staff with numerous e-mail each day, consider sending one large e-mail each week.

When you are tempted to send an e-mail to your entire staff, consider whether or not they need to know the information immediately or if it can wait a few days. If it can wait, write yourself a reminder. By the end of the week, you will probably have several items to be included. Tailor the content to your own situation; in addition to those items on your list, consider reviewing your schedule for the upcoming week, programs happening at your branch in the upcoming week, and community groups meeting at the branch in the upcoming week.

STAFF MEETINGS

Have the right kind of meetings; if well utilized, they are great for encouraging discussion and exchanging ideas. Staff meetings are too often used as a place to make general announcements. It is difficult to get staff together in one place; take advantage of it by leading discussions of big-picture topics. There are other ways to make general announcements. Consider these basic guidelines:

- Very brief morning meetings are a great way to touch base before opening, highlight what will be happening that day, and ensure that everyone is on the same page.
- Individual meetings are the best way to discuss performance and projects with staff members. Set up a schedule and stick to it.
- Position a dry-erase board near the employee entrance so staff can see it when they arrive. Record items that came up in your morning meeting or critical information staff need to know as soon as their shift begins; this is more effective than e-mail.
- A staff blog is a good way to encourage discussion, and a branch wiki is an effective way to consolidate information.

Both new and experienced managers would agree that managing a branch library offers exciting opportunities and unique challenges. From offering programs that focus on the specific needs of your neighborhood to developing relationships with members of your local community, the rewards of branch librarianship can be great. By realizing the challenges of branch management and addressing them, you can go a long way toward solidifying your branch's place as a centerpiece of your neighborhood.

PART II
Running a Library

11

ASSURE-ING YOUR COLLECTION

Roxanne Myers Spencer and Barbara Fiehn

THE ASSURE model of instructional design provides a collection management framework. This model is flexible enough to be adapted for all libraries. As a goal-based model, it provides direction for all functions and levels of staff.

ASSURE is an acronym for an instructional design model used for developing and refining instruction.[1] Each letter represents a task in planning for instruction:

ASSURE Model

Analyze learners

State learning objectives

Select methods, media, and materials

Utilize methods, media, and materials

Require learner participation

Evaluate and revise

Taking an instructional design model out of its original context and applying it to library collection management may seem odd, but it is worth exploring. ASSURE can provide a workable structure for building, analyzing, evaluating, and maintaining library collections:

ASSURE Adapted to Collection Management

Analyze users

State collection objectives

Select methods, media, materials, or format

Utilize selection and deselection methods, media, materials, or format

Recruit library participation

Evaluate and revise regularly

ASSURE FOR COLLECTION MANAGEMENT: Step by Step
Analyze Users

Despite the familiarity that develops between staff and frequent patrons, library users are not a constant population. Viewed in a collection management context, librarians should consider general user characteristics as well as the specific or unique aspects of user populations: What language or literacy barriers exist? How popular is fiction versus nonfiction? Among student populations, which materials are most popular? Other considerations are learning styles, popular formats, and leisure tastes.

Establishing thumbnail overviews of library patrons can provide helpful information on evolving library clientele. Use on-site or virtual suggestion boxes, exit surveys, or one-question queries. Formal community surveys require planning and encumber funds and staff time. Analyzing current and potential users assures that dollars are spent effectively.

State Collection Objectives

As library communities change, collection requirements change. Keeping pace with technology, formats, and patron preferences is an ever-present challenge. Stating collection objectives clarifies the library's mission and services on the basis of an understanding of the library's users. It also provides focus for staff who are selecting materials. Objectives can be measured and flexible and should be reexamined periodically. Alignment between goals and users reduces purchase errors.

Collection mapping—examining and evaluating the collection—helps librarians assess where the collection is weak or does not meet patron needs.[2] When time is short, utilize readily available data, such as in-house use and circulation statistics, to guide evaluation and selection processes.[3]

Select Methods, Media, Materials, or Format

New librarians can be overwhelmed by the multitude of selection resources. Selectors are bombarded by publisher offerings, patron requests, and recommendations in a multiplicity of formats and prices. No collection budget can keep up with the demand or hype associated with the next big title or format. Libraries face an increasingly complex set of demands for delivery of new materials. Devising an inclusive selection process is an opportunity to increase the library's visibility.

Support for literacy and learning styles applies to all library collections. Librarians can provide literacy support by addressing learning styles and exploring new formats and media.

Academic librarians will be familiar with the Research Libraries Group's system of five collection levels.[4] These levels, simplified and adapted below, can be used by most libraries to address selection scope:

Simplified RLG Selection Scope

> 0 Out of: Library does not collect at this level; no materials are purchased on this subject.

> 1 Minimal level: Basic works in a subject only.

> 2 Basic information level: Up-to-date information that introduces a subject and expands to provide information on the variety of topics.

> 3 Comprehensive level: Special collections address collecting local history, authors, etc.

Utilize Selection and Weeding Methods, Media, Materials, or Format

All libraries benefit from utilizing varied services and media. Topical book talks, reading clubs, licensed movie performances, and traveling exhibitions may help bring in new patrons. The impact of displays cannot be underestimated in boosting library circulation. An experiment at the Lafayette (Colorado) Public Library showed an increase in circulation of fiction titles by 90 percent and nonfiction by 25 percent when selected duplicate titles were displayed.[5]

The bookstore model of library layout has been a popular template because of the emphasis on higher visibility of materials. This model can be adapted even when extensive remodeling is not an option.

Recruit Library Participation

In the original ASSURE model, this step is "require learner participation." Our adaptation is "recruit library participation." This is particularly important to solo librarians. Address this step by engaging the community. To encourage active participation, recruit Friends groups, students, parents, teachers, and other community members for tasks, such as creating displays or monitoring local newspaper reviews, that do not require specialized library training.

Evaluate and Revise

Continuous evaluation and revision are essential. Assess the model through periodic examination of the processes and procedures:

- Maintain logs: Keep running lists of concerns and issues that arise.
- Chart successes: Gain feedback from staff and patrons via surveys, spot interviews, suggestion boxes, or intranet blogs.
- Check circulation statistics and reference logs for changes in library use patterns.
- Review the six ASSURE steps monthly and modify as needed.

The six steps of the ASSURE model create an organized system for collection management. Each step can be followed by solo librarians or libraries with staff, providing a flexible structure for examining and developing standardized tasks. The ASSURE model provides each participant with clear direction and opportunities to contribute to building and maintaining a useful library collection.

Selected Resources

American Library Association. 2009. ALA library fact sheet 7: Video and copyright. www.lita.org/ala/professionalresources/libfactsheets/alalibraryfactsheet07.cfm.

Bradburn, Frances Bryant. 1999. *Output Measures for School Library Media Programs.* New York: Neal-Schuman.
    User-friendly and useful how-to book about gathering and using evaluation data.

Burgett, James, John Haar, and Linda L. Phillips. 2004. *Collaborative Collection Development: A Practical Guide for Your Library.* Chicago: American Library Association.
    Theoretical principles along with real-world strategies for developing collaborative work.

Laughlin, Sara. 2003. *The Library's Continuous Improvement Field Book: 29 Ready-to-Use Tools.* Chicago: American Library Association.
    This guide applies quality management concepts to make library processes more effective.

Rubin, Rhea Joyce. 2005. *Demonstrating Results: Using Outcome Measurement in Your Library.* Chicago: American Library Association
    An information-gathering toolkit to provide a higher, more responsive level of service.

Notes

1. Sharon E. Smaldino, Deborah L. Lowther, and James D. Russell, *Instructional Technology and Media for Learning* (Upper Saddle River, N.J.: Pearson Merrill Prentice Hall, 2008).
2. David V. Loertscher. "Collection Mapping: An Evaluation Strategy for Collection Development," *Drexel Library Quarterly* 21, no. 2 (1985): 9–21.
3. Alice Crosetto, Laura Kinner, and Lucy Duhon, "Assessment in a Tight Time Frame: Using Readily Available Data to Evaluate Your Collection," *Collection Management* 33, nos. 1–2 (2008.): 29–50, http://pdfserve.informaworld.com/551022_788638144_903761953.pdf.
4. Library of Congress, *Cataloging and Acquisitions: Collecting Levels,* www.loc.gov/acq/devpol/cpc.html.
5. Michele Seipp, Sandra Lindberg, and Keith Curry Lance, "Book Displays Increase Fiction Circulation over 90%, Non-Fiction Circulation 25%," *Fast Facts: Recent Statistics from the Library Research Service,* no. 184 (2002).

12

BILLY CLUB: A MODEL FOR DEALING WITH UNRETURNED LIBRARY MATERIALS

Suzann Holland

THE FAILURE to return library materials constitutes theft of municipal property. Should you fail to deal with it aggressively, you encourage more of the same. Remember that the core mission of a library is to provide access to information. If one patron is allowed to retain materials permanently, every other patron is denied access to those materials until they are replaced. Replacing unreturned materials means less money for additional and newer materials for the patrons; the overall quality of the collection goes down as a result of the actions of a few. Do not allow scofflaws that much control over library operations. Whether or not you choose to utilize the Billy Club model presented below, do something.

PRELIMINARY ACTIONS

Begin your materials recovery program with the understanding that this is a time-consuming process. Time spent on the Billy Club process must be regular—a sporadic effort is not as effective and leads to wasted resources. Depending on the size of your library, you may choose to handle all aspects of the program personally or to delegate part of it to others. Try to limit the number of parties involved to avoid confusion.

Research the law that applies to your library. Most states address the theft of library materials within the code. You may also have a relevant municipal ordinance. If no specific law regarding library materials is on the books, it can still be considered a criminal matter under the standard theft laws.

With a copy of the applicable law in hand, find a partner organization. Typically, you will work with either the police or the county attorney's office. Try to set up a meeting that includes a representative of each potential entity. To avoid that "police looking for an overdue book" assumption, make it clear that the program is intended for serious cases. Let potential partner organizations offer input and suggestions.

Once you have secured the tentative cooperation of law enforcement, create a draft policy to take to the library board. You may create an entirely new policy, or perhaps you will amend an existing one with a new section. The policy should clearly lay out the scope of the program. Include the following:

- *Minimum for legal action.* This might be a dollar amount of value or perhaps a certain number of items. If the items in question fall below the minimum, deal with them quickly and bill the patron's card.

- *How to handle minors.* At what age will you contact a minor directly rather than the parents? Get professional advice from your city or county attorney on this. You do not want to send dunning letters to a 6-year-old child or to the parents of a 17-year-old teenager. Confidentiality is also a major factor.
- *What happens afterward.* If you have to resort to law enforcement to get your materials back, will privileges be reinstated? Will the patron be charged for the associated costs, such as certified mailing expenses?

Make sure each component of the policy is in accordance with the law. For example, if your state code specifies that materials are being illegally held at 90 days past the due date, make sure your policy does not commence the materials recovery procedure at 60 days. With a board-approved policy in hand, you are ready to begin. Follow the steps noted below, adapting them for your situation. Be sure to follow the same steps with all patrons, unless you have different procedures for minors.

SUGGESTED STEPS AT A GLANCE

1. Identify patrons. Refer to regularly scheduled reports to determine your Billy Club roster. For instance, if your criteria are $100 worth of items at least 90 days overdue, get a report of patrons who meet those criteria on the first day of each month.

2. Begin tracking Billy Club patrons. You may choose to use a spreadsheet, a database, or a retro index card solution. Because there are multiple steps in the process, you need to know where each Billy Clubber is in the process. Your chosen tracking system ensures that you know what needs to be done and when to do it.

3. Send your first letter to the patron (see Sample Letter). The purpose of the initial letter is twofold: to encourage the patron to return the materials without further action, and to verify the mailing address. The letter states that the patron has ten days to return the items in question. Wait fifteen days before proceeding to step 4. If your letter is returned to sender, go directly to step 6.

4. Send a certified letter with a return receipt to the patron. You will be able to prove later that the patron received the letter and failed to act on it. Check the law in your state; some require that the restricted delivery option be used. This letter is exactly the same as the original letter but is dated later. Wait fifteen days before proceeding to step 5.

5. Write the materials off. Alter the records as needed in your system so the missing items are not checked in if later returned. Either reorder or delete each item. They cannot be returned in lieu of payment from this point forward.

6. Turn the matter over to law enforcement with supporting documentation: copies of all mailed letters, including any returned mail; identifying information about the patron in question, such as a driver's license number; and itemization of unreturned items including titles, due dates, and replacement costs.

7. Refer affected patrons to partner organization if they call. The matter is out of your hands. If the patron offers to pay in full, take the money and provide a receipt stapled to your business card. The patron will need to deal with the partner organization.

SAMPLE LETTER

Dear Patron:

I am writing to inform you that you have 10 days from the receipt of this letter to return the following materials in good condition to the Anytown Public Library:

DVD—*Harry Potter and the Sorcerer's Stone*, due 2/16/2009
Book on CD—*Going Rogue*, due 2/13/2009
Book—*The Appeal*, due 2/13/2009

Alternatively, you may pay the full replacement costs due for these items, in the amount of $83.91.

If you do not resolve this matter within the time specified above, be advised that this will be reported to the police as a theft.

Celeste Collins, Director

ADDITIONAL TIPS

Any of the following tips may be applicable in your situation:

- Hold the patron responsible for an entire multipart item if the checked-out item cannot be replaced individually. For example, if a patron checks out a single disc of *Desperate Housewives: The Complete First Season*, charge the replacement cost for the whole season.
- Find as many ways to automate the process as you can. Letter templates, labels, a good tracking system—they are important tools.
- Consider photocopying a photo ID as a part of the card registration procedure.

- Add wording to your card application that notifies the patron of the law; try something like "I understand that failure to return library materials within 90 days of the due date constitutes theft under Iowa law."
- If a patron requests a payment plan, put it in writing with both a schedule and the patron's signature. Include wording that the plan must be followed or the issue will become a matter for the partner organization.
- Accept only cash payment in full if the patron comes to you after being contacted by the partner organization.

13

COLLABORATION FOR LIBRARY COLLECTION ACQUISITION

Lorette S. J. Weldon

THIS "HOW-TO" chapter can help you develop an acquisitions program that feeds documents and other items into a library collection. Through carefully defined teamwork and collaboration within the library's staff and with other organizations, this method convenes different groups and individuals for information exchange, identifies the big issues, and provides valuable, different perspectives on them.

WHAT ARE THEY THINKING?

Begin by sending out a feedback survey to find out if the patrons want more that your collection contains. This allows patrons to tell you if they have received information or documents that answered their questions. The survey functions as a tool to help you identify relevant documents that reflect current and future interests of the patrons for the collection.

When I applied this program in my library, I used open-ended questions so that patrons were freer to respond. If the questions allow for more of a response than "yes" or "no," patrons can take better advantage of the chance to be heard. Patrons do realize that this will help them with future research needs. The following are the process and basic questions that helped me get a better picture of what the patrons wanted:

1. Create a survey through Survey Monkey (www.surveymonkey.com).

2. Select the participants from the membership and send them surveys; or create e-mail messages to them with a link to electronic versions of the survey.

3. Receive responses and catalog the open-ended responses by answering the following questions:

   - *What* is happening?
   - *How* did X or Y answer the question?
   - *Who* answered the question?
   - *Where* did the request get answered (e-mail, phone, etc)?
   - *When* did it happen?

SAMPLE SURVEY

Your survey will benefit from questions such as the following, but adapt them to suit your own library situation:

1. Before responding to this survey, were you aware of the existence of the library?

2. Have you personally used the services of the library or had someone else use the services of the library on your behalf?

3. How did you contact the library to ask for research help?

4. Were you able to obtain the information you were seeking?

5. I am aware that the library offers [answer yes or no]

   - webinars for patrons on a range of topics
   - a librarian who answers questions about a range of topics
   - an online library for sharing documents

6. Do you have documents that you are willing to share with the library collection? [answer yes or no]

7. Do you find the discussion list helpful?

8. List three things the library typically does very well.

9. List three things the library could do much better.

GO BACK HOME

Another way to find out what the collection lacks in terms of patron requests is to have an informal retreat with the researchers on staff in your library. I found that through biweekly lunchtime retreats I could recruit members for a special team who could contribute past, present, and future "lived experiences" of staff in the research study areas of the library. This kind of team can help you assess the library for missing elements related to their area of study.

Each member of the team is tasked to produce their findings in a concisely written, short brief. The results can be matched across several library collections in your area (location and subject specialty), including private, government, academic, and information industry sectors.

The costs of this collaborative approach fall naturally into two parts. Internal costs include office supplies, postage, telephone bills, equipment leasing and maintenance, travel expenses, acquisitions, and subscriptions for online databases and journals. Typical external costs might cover collecting benchmarks for subject areas, programs and services that provide patrons a framework for understanding the subject areas of the collection, Trends Tracker pertaining to the subject area, and convening sub-groups of patrons for information exchange.

14

COMMUNITY PARTNERSHIPS: THE KEY TO PROVIDING PROGRAMS IN A RECESSION

Ashanti White

LIBRARIES, LIKE businesses, are affected by the recession, but as we have witnessed in prior recessions individuals rely on institutions to maintain cultural development, conduct career and educational services, and form social bonds. During the Great Depression, library use burgeoned. A study conducted by the Massachusetts Board of Library Commissioners titled "What Happened to Public Libraries during the Great Depression?" found that the use of public libraries grew in unprecedented numbers from 1930 to 1931, with a majority of libraries reporting from a 10 to 40 percent increase in circulation for 1932, several reporting a 60–80 percent increase, and a few 100 percent and more. A librarian interviewed at the time commented: "Reading rooms have been crowded. The number of books borrowed in 1932 exceeded 31 million volumes, nearly 8.5 million more than in 1930."[1]

The current recession is no different. From 2008, when the current recession began, to 2009, checkouts of books, CDs, and DVDs increased 15 percent at the main library in Modesto, California. In Boulder, Colorado, circulation of job-hunting materials was up 14 percent, and usage of the Newark Public Library in New Jersey was up 17 percent during the same period. Library card requests increased 27 percent in the last half of 2008 in San Francisco.[2] In a survey conducted for the 2010 State of the Library Report, ALA found that 43 percent of respondents ages 18–24 and 32 percent of those ages 35–44 increased their use of the public library in the second half of 2009. Furthermore, 34 percent of those who were employed and 24 percent of the unemployed reported increasing overall use of the public library.[3]

Such accelerated usage would normally motivate libraries to increase their efforts and resources for summer reading programs, computer training, and language classes that support the literary, educational, and recreational needs of customers, but the recession has negatively impacted libraries as well, and these programs are among the first cut during financially challenging times. Still, budget cuts do not necessarily imply that customers have to do without these services. Library administrators simply have to develop creative methods of tackling these issues. One tactic that has proved successful is the formulation of community partnerships. By continuing with and seeking to form partnerships with schools, government agencies, and other organizations, libraries can ensure that helpful programs are still provided.

MORE THAN OUTREACH

Collaborations are as rooted in library history as lending practices. For years, librarians have been involved in working with community agencies to deliver service primarily through traditional outreach programs. However, librarians must understand that community partnerships are more encompassing than outreach. Outreach occurs when libraries present their programs and materials in locations other than their branches. Outreach services also provide information and deliver materials to participating homeless facilities, nursing homes, and individuals who are permanently or temporarily unable to get to a library. Conversely, community partnership involves a formal agreement between two or more agencies to provide mutual support in attaining a common goal.[4] Additionally, outreach relies heavily on the resources of the library; often, the other organization simply acts as publicity or provides the venue.

> **QUICK TIP**
> Consistency is key. For a series of programs, such as English or computer classes, libraries should strive for constant attendance, not an initially large attendance that dwindles in subsequent weeks. Constant participation and attendance are signs of success.

Let us compare models of the two. Outreach may involve a few librarians going to a high school to sign kids up for library cards; little collaboration is involved. Community partnership requires cooperation.[5] A successful example would be the library planning programs, such as book discussions, around the ninth-grade English curriculum. The school could assist by providing relevant study guides and a teacher or school librarian as moderator. The activity engages students, who can gain insight into their readings, and the school and library promote interest in literacy. The most important aspect in partnerships is sustainability; long-term partnerships should be the goal, since this allows the library to improve its services while establishing credibility as a community institution.

REEVALUATING NEEDS

Times of financial hardship also allow libraries to reevaluate the nature of their programs, perhaps exposing superfluous or frivolous programs that were established when times were better. Although no customer group is more or less important than another, libraries have to target the demographics of their customers, determining what programs they need and what goals they would like to achieve in providing these programs. Furthermore, they must determine their largest customer groups, which groups regularly support library events, and the staff time and resources needed to provide programs for those groups. It would be nonsensical for a system with few teenage customers and a large Hispanic base to use partner volunteers for teen events with lackluster results when those volunteers could teach conversational English sessions that many Spanish speakers would consistently attend.

LIMITLESS POSSIBILITIES

One of the greatest aspects of community partnerships is that organizations and agencies are so vast that libraries are largely unlimited in the types of programs they can provide. Recessions mark an increase in citizens conducting job searches, updating their resumes, or transitioning into new careers. This is an optimal opportunity for libraries to build relationships with nonprofit business centers. A professional from the center can lead sessions on resume building or interviewing. The center can provide helpful handouts, and library workers can direct individuals who require additional information to the center. Studies have proved that children's programs develop literacy skills that are pertinent to academic success. Moreover, those programs are among the most popular of public library events. Public librarians can seek to establish a partnership with the elementary education department of the local college to develop children's programs. Not only does the library benefit, the customers and students, who by state laws must have a specific number of hours in their fields, benefit.

Libraries can even partner with other libraries. Greensboro Public Library has partnered with the University of North Carolina at Greensboro's Jackson Library for "One City One Book." Hosted biannually, the citywide reading project provides a host of events, including discussions and Friends of the Library readings that focus on a particular title and its themes. With possibilities to collaborate with churches, mentoring groups, schools, volunteer organizations, and government agencies, the library can fulfill the informational and practical needs of the community.

POSSIBLE PARTNERS

- charity organizations
- churches and faith-based groups
- community centers
- government agencies
- high schools
- literary councils
- museums
- university departments

Although outreach is entrenched in many library policies, libraries have to go a step further to form community partnerships that are mutually beneficial to the partner organizations as well as the customers. The current recession makes collaboration with other organizations a near necessity for libraries that hope to continue providing programs to their customers despite dwindling resources. By identifying the needs of the library, thinking creatively, and remaining dedicated to the goal of satisfying customers and partners, libraries will not only maintain their relevance but firmly establish their standing in the community.

Notes

1. "What Happened to Public Libraries during the Great Depression?" Massachusetts Board of Library Commissioners, 2009, http://mblc.state.ma.us/grants/state_aid/blog/statistics/what-happened-to-public-libraries-during-the-great-depression.
2. "The State of American Libraries," *American Library Association*, 2009, www.ala.org/ala/newspresscenter/mediapresscenter/presskits/2009stateofamericas libraries/2009statehome.cfm.
3. "The State of American Libraries," *American Library Association*, 2010, www.ala.org/ala/newspresscenter/mediapresscenter/americaslibraries/ALA_Report_2010-ATI001-NEW1.pdf.
4. Carolyn Bourke, "Public Libraries: Partnerships, Funding, and Relevance," *Aplis*, September 2007, 137–38.
5. "Information Literacy Community Partnerships Toolkit." ALA *Special Presidential Committee on Information Literacy*, 2001, http://library.austincc.edu/presentations/CommunityPartnerships.

15

CVL LEADS: MENTORSHIP AND LEADERSHIP

Robin Shader

CHATTAHOOCHEE VALLEY (Georgia) Libraries Leadership and Development Sessions—or CVL Leads!—is a two-year in-house leadership program that began in September 2009. The program was developed with the following organizational goals in mind:

- prepare our current staff for future leadership positions
- foster a learning environment
- involve more nonmanagement staff in problem-solving projects
- encourage staff to pursue an MLS
- encourage protégé/mentor relationships

PLANNING

Deciding which organizational goals to address allowed us to decide which target group to include in the training. You may wish to develop new librarians, new supervisors, or some other category of staff. Another decision is whether to allow part-time staff to participate. The CVL Leads! program requires participants to attend one session per month, plus meet regularly with their mentor. Assigned projects require hours of work. Decide whether part-timers in your library have the time to participate fully. At CVL, we wanted to provide development training to staff members who showed interest and potential in order to create more opportunities to hire and promote from within, so we invited all staff members to apply. Out of eleven applicants, five non-MLS staff members were selected.

START WITH MEASURABLE OBJECTIVES

Take the time to identify learning objectives that can be measured. This helps you focus training efforts and makes it possible to determine whether the program was successful.

Plan your programs with your desired results in mind. Prior to the start of the CVL Leads! program, we defined measurable objectives to focus training efforts and to make it possible to determine whether the program was successful. For example, one objective is to develop staff so that we can hire from within. An obvious way to measure this is to track how many participants obtain promotions within three years.

Programs and projects were developed to address the following topics: customer service, leadership and supervision, project management, technology in libraries, and standards and best practices. Additionally, there is an independent project component so participants can pursue projects of particular interest that may not be covered during regular sessions.

BUDGET

The WebJunction report "Staff Training in Public Libraries: 2007 Fact Sheet" provided survey results from public libraries that offered training programs at that time.[1] This report indicated that conference and face-to-face training were considered the most effective training options. With this in mind, CVL Leads! is designed to include mostly face-to-face training and requires participants to attend a national conference. An annual budget of $7,500 covers the following costs:

- paid ALA membership for each of the five participants
- one paid library-related national conference of their choice
- selected books for required reading
- workshop attendance (outside the library)
- speakers/trainers (cost of trainers coming to the library)
- program supplies (journals, binders, etc.)

The bulk of the budget is spent on conference attendance and presenters. If funding is an issue, national conferences can be replaced with state or regional meetings, and sessions facilitated by in-house staff can replace outside trainers. Utilize the expertise in your region and do not limit your trainers to people who are strictly library trainers. Survey agencies in your service area to determine which ones provide training relevant to the library environment. Network with your state library leaders and identify trainers in nearby libraries. Many librarians would be honored to be invited to your library to offer training and may charge only expenses. We have been able to provide top-notch training at a reasonable cost by utilizing the outstanding talent in our region.

PROGRAM COORDINATOR

You need a program coordinator to oversee the program. The program coordinator is responsible for scheduling and evaluating sessions, meeting with participants and mentors to assess the success of the relationships, managing the program budget, and presenting some of the sessions. This person is also the liaison to the administration and keeps them informed of the progress of the group.

COMPETITIVE APPLICATION PROCESS

We required interested staff members to complete an application listing their reasons for applying to the program, what they hoped to learn, previous volunteer experience, and career goals. Completed applications, with names removed, were given to the administrative team for ranking. Scores were totaled, and the five highest ranked scores became the first CVL Leads! class.

GROWING OUR OWN

The program is designed to be two years in duration in order for the participants to become fully involved in the projects assigned. Our goal is not only to provide leadership and management theories but to enable participants to put these theories to use to help solve current library problems. Involving the participants in actual library projects enhances their learning and develops a larger pool of staff members who can be counted on later to manage projects. These experiences better prepare participants to fill management positions that become vacant, This is how we grow our own.

Mentors were assigned to give each participant help with assignments, provide advice, and help them learn about and navigate the organization. Each participant was required to name, in the application, up to three people who they would like to be their mentor. The mentorship component reinforces the value of seeking mentors and taking advantage of the human resources available within and outside the organization. Participants are encouraged to network and seek out mentors everywhere. When assigning mentors, keep in mind the following:

DON'T REINVENT THE WHEEL
Review the literature on the many successful leadership programs out there. Use available resources to build a program that best benefits your organization.

- Participant/mentor relationships do not always succeed. Be prepared to dissolve the partnership if it does not work out.

- Consider whether to allow a supervisor, or someone in that reporting line, to be a mentor. Allowing a participant to select her supervisor's boss to be a mentor could cause tension between some of the parties involved.
- Make sure the mentor has the time to devote to meeting with the participant regularly. We asked participants and mentors to sign a contract acknowledging the requirements.

ORIENTATION

The first program was a two-hour orientation attended by the participants and their mentors and facilitated by the program coordinator. Program goals were discussed and each participant spent time talking with her mentor. A list of discussion starter questions was provided to the pairs, who were given thirty minutes to talk. An assignment during orientation was to create a list of personal learning objectives. These will be used to develop future programs to ensure a valuable experience for all participants.

INDEPENDENT PROJECT

During the course of the program, participants must complete an independent project of their choosing. This could be publishing an article, presenting a program at a conference, managing a library project, among other possibilities. The project must be approved by the program coordinator. The independent project encourages participants to explore topics they are interested in, then share what they have learned with their colleagues.

RESULTS

The first CVL Leads! project was to plan our Staff In-Service Day for 127 employees. This took several months and involved identifying presenters and completing contracts, budgeting, managing logistics, creating and compiling staff registrations, arranging for food, and acquiring raffle prizes and giveaways for staff. Post-program surveys were compiled and will be used to improve next year's program. One member of the group was elected project manager. This project allowed the group to get to know each other and gave them experience working with widely different work styles. They now have project management experience from which they can draw in the future.

The program is only in its first year but has already achieved some of its goals. We have increased training for all library staff and increased involvement of nonmanagement staff in library projects and problem solving. Four of the five members have indicated an interest in obtaining a library degree. One member attended the PLA conference and another will attend and copresent a program during the Computers in Libraries conference.

CVL Leaders are involved, encouraged, and engaged in both local library issues and the profession. A commitment to growing our own will benefit our library and the greater library community.

Note
1. WebJunction, "Staff Training in Public Libraries: 2007 Fact Sheet," http://ia.webjunc
tion.org/c/document_library/get_file?folderId=455478&name=DLFE-14557.pdf.

16

HOW TO MANAGE A STUDENT-CENTRIC LIBRARY SERVICE FOR NONTRADITIONAL USERS

Seamus Scanlon

THE CENTER for Worker Education (CWE) in New York City offers a BA in inter-disciplinary studies, a BS in early childhood education, and an MA in studies of the Americas. It was established in the 1970s by the trade unions in New York so that members could attend college in the evenings and on weekends. Traditional college undergraduate courses in the main are daytime affairs, which creates barriers of access for workers who wish to acquire a college education. Once they are in the world of work with multiple financial and other commitments, the daytime regime of most college courses is a major impediment because it would mean eschewing their income to attend classes.

Thus the ethos of CWE from the 1970s was fashioned by the nontraditional student intake. The demographics of the intake cohort has widened from the original union membership and been augmented by homemakers, part-time workers, retirees, and others with fractured school attendance. Classes are still scheduled for the evenings and Saturdays to facilitate their schedules.

CWE STYLE

The emphasis at CWE is close attention to student needs, whether in the classroom, in advising sessions, or in the corridors where faculty, staff, and students encounter each other on a daily basis. The physical layout of the institution (seventh floor of the Cunard Building in Lower Manhattan) and scale of operations (ten faculty, seventy adjuncts, and 750 students) make it much easier to establish bonds between faculty/staff and students. Individual attention is the essence of the CWE style (as I brand it) and is palpable from all staff: front of desk, security, custodians, advisors, faculty, adjuncts, chair, dean, and, since 2008, librarian. When I started as that librarian, I adopted the "style," and it blended naturally with the student-centric library style I was able to implement.

TYPICAL PROBLEMS FACED BY NONTRADITIONAL STUDENTS

Students at CWE face problems typical of nontraditional students anywhere:

- more mature intake (25 years plus) than the City College of New York main campus (18 years), so longer out of formal education
- busier, more commitments, shorter burst of time on campus
- some returning to college decades after leaving college
- some going to college for the first time decades after leaving high school
- less familiar with purpose and format of research papers, citations, footnotes
- uninformed about information technology, e-mail, attachments, embedding videos, passwords, databases, flash drives, temp directories, saving work, Blackboard

KEYS TO DEVELOPING A STUDENT-CENTRIC STYLE

Immediate Resolution of Problems

Whether the library is confronted by minor issues (uncomfortable seating) or serious issues (information technology, off-campus access, printing, etc.), the key to solving the problem is often the resolve of the librarian. Once the student-centric ethos is in effect, proactive and quick-response service is self-perpetuating. One feeds the other.

Any issue that impedes students' learning experience detracts from their rights as fee payers expecting a premier service; it also tarnishes the standing of the library and parent institution. The converse is also true in that rapid response to any issue unblocks barriers quickly, adds to the air of competence and professionalism in the library, and generates goodwill among students, who know that when issues arise they will be resolved. One needs to prioritize issues, of course; information technology generally outweighs seating comfort, for instance, but resolution of all issues contributes to the quality of the student-centric service.

Welcoming Atmosphere

Promote a conducive learning environment for students who may be anxious about their nascent library skills. Supply positive reinforcement of students' developing skills, demystify the research paper process, and treat students as equals in the learning process.

Individual Attention

One-on-one training and individual interaction are always the optimum route for novice library users. Working through an issue with a student in an individual tutorial session has more effect than, for example, performing the catalog search for them or expecting them to follow verbal explanations. Although more time consuming, personal training reaps great benefits, including giving students immediate reinforcement when they see they can perform a task effectively and efficiently. This boosts their confidence, which in turn makes them more adventurous and more willing to explore other databases and resources.

Special Attention

Some older students may have little skill with computers, e-mail, and the array of user name and password combinations for access to blogs, Blackboard, and the institution's portal as well as the more mundane negotiation of Microsoft Office applications or the Statistical Package for the Social Sciences—all needed to complete assignments efficiently. This means you have to give them more help and over an extended period. These issues fall outside the usual remit of library service, but it remains part of the information stream so at CWE we provide help with any software issue that is raised.

Repeat Business

We encourage repeat visits by telling students to be certain to come back if they have a problem. We hand out business cards, tell them to contact us, and respond quickly to messages left by e-mail or phone. Once students sense that they are welcome in the library, they tend to return often.

WHY A STUDENT–CENTRIC APPROACH WORKS AT THE CWE LIBRARY

- CWE style and library style match closely.
- Rapid response to high-impact problems like database access or barcode validation makes a significant difference to the quality of service.
- The student-centric philosophy spurs the library toward excellence. To maintain an excellence rating, the library is invested in unraveling any issue that might stymie the library experience.
- Individual attention boosts students' confidence in their own ability.
- Being proactive in anticipating and observing students' difficulties demonstrates the professionalism of the library service.
- We elicit the needs of students through probing questions, looking at the syllabus together, and so forth.
- Suggesting alternatives to purchasing texts are always appreciated by students. (The City University of New York Libraries Inter-Campus Service and interlibrary loan are both free.)
- Overcoming students' shyness with regard to information technology know-how transforms their ability to complete assignments and bolster grades.
- Going beyond an original query shows commitment to the long haul, not just quick-fix solutions.
- Making students feel at ease and treated as equals bolsters their confidence to ask further questions because they know they will receive attention.

- Demystifying the research process shows students that they can complete tasks easily and on time.
- Providing worked examples during workshops gives valuable hands-on experience.
- Handing out business cards with contact details provides students an easy way to make contact.
- Responding to e-mails and phone calls in a timely manner solves problems for students and elicits favorable comments.
- Being courteous and listening closely are respectful and show parity of esteem.
- We have developed a nonthreatening and supportive library atmosphere—no job too big or too small.

17

MANAGING OVERNIGHT

Ken Johnson and Susan Jennings

THE BEST thing a library can be is open," said Michael Freeman, then director of Haverford College in Pennsylvania, who offered this interesting comment during an exchange of ideas on the merits of offering 24-hour library services.[1] Appalachian State University's Belk Library and Information Commons recently converted to a 24-hour facility five nights weekly between Sunday and Friday night. The following case study outlines our successful change to this operational model, including our observations on staffing, services, and security.

TRANSITIONAL PHASES

Our learning and research services team found the transition to a 24-hour facility a challenging process. We worked diligently to overcome moderate staff resistance and to make the changes successful and sustainable. Now that we have worked through the process, library personnel agree that being open is indeed the best thing.

Phase One: Setting the Stage (2005)

The process began in June 2005 when we moved into a new library and information commons that included an expanded number of new computers, wireless access, new services, and more group study rooms. We extended the closing hour on school nights from midnight to 2 a.m. The campus student government association (SGA) adopted an initiative to support the effort to extend library hours at the new facility. The university librarian committed herself to work with the SGA to push for funding from the university administration to cover the associated costs.

Phase Two: Initial Steps (2006/07)

In working with SGA we learned that students wanted computer access and a study space in the library. Since we had little idea of demand, we decided first to open the atrium and coffee shop areas 24/5. Our building design allowed us to lock the main library areas while still allowing access to the atrium and coffee shop. The coffee shop made for an inviting study space with comfortable seating, tables, and sixteen computer workstations. At the 2 a.m. closing time, night staffers asked students to move to the atrium/ coffee shop area so they could lock down the rest of the building. We hired one private security guard to monitor the area overnight. The guard tallied hourly head counts and the type of student activity, including using computers, studying, sleeping, and socializing.

INVOLVE THESE KEY STAKEHOLDERS

- *library administration*
- *library staff*
- *student government association*
- *university police*
- *university administration*

Phase Three: Open during Exams (2008/09)

In January 2008, we implemented a plan to stay open 24/5 for ten days during mid-term exams and fifteen days leading up to and during final exams. All library personnel departed at 2 a.m. We increased the private security coverage to a four-person team that patrolled the building from 11 p.m. until 7:30 a.m., when regular staff returned. The security team continued to tally hourly head counts. Additionally, the guards checked everyone for student identification and asked those without student identification to leave the building. In the interest of student safety, we also decided to close all group study rooms at 2 a.m.

Phase Four: 24/5 Library Facility (late 2009 to present)

After persistent lobbying of university administrators by SGA and the university librarian, the university granted the library $100,000 in supplemental money from the tuition increase pool of funds. This money allowed the library to become a 24/5 facility during fall and spring semesters. We expanded the facility operations model from phase three to cover the entire semester.

STAFFING AND SERVICES

Our biggest breakthrough occurred during the transitional phases when the university librarian and the coordinator of public services resolved to turn over the building to the private security team and to close circulation and reference services at 2 a.m. This solution essentially converted the library into a large computer lab and study space.

The SGA advised us throughout that students were willing to sacrifice traditional library services during the overnight hours. Our experience during phase three proved the SGA correct. We have had no requests to provide reference services overnight, and we utilize our 3M self-checkout unit to handle the small circulation demand.

By employing the private security team, we overcame much of the resistance and staff turnover among three library evening and night supervisors. During phases one and two, the library administration strongly considered the possibility of converting the night supervisors to third-shift employees. Positions turned over four times during this period due, in part, to potential changes in job hours. With the current operational model in place, the night supervisors seem more engaged in their work. Although we cannot attribute this engagement entirely to the new operational model, we can observe that we have had no turnover among night supervisors since late 2008.

SECURITY

Contracting a private security team proved to be a sensible step that has developed into an effective working arrangement. Our facility is approximately 165,000 square feet on five floors. The four-person security team walks the floors regularly and records head counts and activity each hour.

Early on, we consulted with senior university police officers to make sure they were comfortable with a private security team in the library. We also worked to make certain the university police would provide timely backup assistance for the security team. Both efforts have been successful. We cannot overemphasize the importance of fostering a positive relationship among the library, the private security team, and the university police force.

Other elements of our building security efforts include an extensive security camera system on all floors, a card swipe system used by students across campus to gain entry to secured campus buildings, and a library staff review each morning to address issues recorded on the security reports.

POLICIES WE PUBLICIZE

Posting our policies prominently on the library website and on the entrance doors has helped to mitigate problems between patrons and the security guards. We also include reminders about safety and respect for the building. Our stated expectations include the following items:

Please Note
- After midnight, the building is open for Appalachian State students, staff, and faculty.
- After midnight, access to the building will require you to swipe your AppCard at the exterior doors.

- Security guards will check your AppCard—anyone not able to present an AppCard will be asked to leave.
- Be conscious of your surroundings, and do not hold the door open for others.
- Please respect the building during the overnight hours by cleaning up after yourself.

Limited Services
- For better security, the study rooms will close at 2 a.m.
- Laptops will be due at 2 a.m. in order to receive automatic updates.
- All service desks will close at 2 a.m.
- The 4th floor will close at the normal time of 10 p.m.

Our successful model has been popular with students and at this point is relatively easy to sustain. Although the transition took over four years to complete, we hope that other libraries may find ways to shorten the process by reviewing our course of action and adapt our model to suit their own campus environment. Our library agrees that the best thing we can be is open. How about your library?

Note
1. Andrew Richard Albanese, "The Best Thing a Library Can Be Is Open," *Library Journal* 130, no. 15 (2005), 42.

18

MANAGING MORE THAN ONE SCHOOL LIBRARY WITH ONE FTE LIBRARIAN

Kris Baughman and Rebecca Marcum Parker

THERE ARE many challenges to managing more than one school library with one FTE librarian or less, especially in an environment where each school has a different daily schedule. We have served two and three schools per year and can offer the following recommendations on the basis of our experiences.

TIME MANAGEMENT, SCHEDULE MANAGEMENT, COMMUNICATION

The challenges of serving three schools at a time are tougher than those for serving two schools, but in each case, communication, time management, and schedule management are priorities. Organizational skills minimize the stress a traveling schedule can create. We use the following helpful tools:

- Microsoft Outlook e-mail and calendars
- Personal mobile device
- Microsoft Office Excel
- Outlook Today Task Lists

Checking e-mail throughout the day is an easy way to be aware of last-minute schedule changes. Another strategy is color-coding building rotations and special events on an Outlook calendar and then synching Outlook to a mobile device. Choose a color to represent each building and highlight nonstudent or nonattendance days in another color. This is helpful in a situation where buildings have different daily schedules. In this age of recession, it is not cost effective to print copies of a calendar with the numerous changes that occur weekly. One suggestion is to allow library clerks permission to view and edit Outlook calendars, so everyone can be on the same page when it comes to scheduling.

One option for managing daily library class schedules is to create an Excel spreadsheet. Color-coding grade levels is a great way to organize the schedule visually. Once the schedule is finalized, it can be stored on a USB drive and e-mailed to staff. Any changes can easily be made, and then the grid can be redistributed. Organizational skills are a must when you are traveling between two schools daily. Keeping a list of tasks in Outlook Today helps prioritize department projects, collaborative projects, and individual library tasks. Even with the vast amount of information technology available, solid communication between librarians and library clerks is important. For us, they are the first line of communication to building staff about schedule changes or resource requests. In a district where staff can keep mobile devices with them, we can send a quick text to the library clerk if we are delayed. If your district does not allow staff to access their mobile devices, then this is not an option.

BUDGET CONCERNS IN A DOWN ECONOMY

In this recession, with cuts in funding and low tax revenues, we are fortunate that our libraries still receive a small budget from the school district. More and more librarians are searching for creative ways to acquire high-quality materials that appeal to diverse populations and hold up to multiple checkouts. Here are some of the creative options for acquiring materials:

- Take advantage of book fair credits.
- Use local vendors who offer percentage discounts.
- Check the local "bulk/salvage" shops for books.
- Accept book donations from staff, parents, and students.
- Ask local vendors for donations.
- Gather free material from conferences or workshops.

Can your district join a library cooperative? Our districts are members of MLNC, the Missouri Library Network Corporation, which provides information services throughout the state, workshops, training, and discounts on a variety of library-related products and services. There is a list of vendors that offer discounts to co-op members. Using the membership code makes ordering from library supply catalogs more cost effective. Shop around for vendors who offer free shipping or free processing on book orders. Talk to your local PTA officers about making a donation to your library. If your school meets the criteria, apply for the RIF (Reading Is Fundamental) program; each student receives a free book, and sometimes extra books are donated to the library, so more students have access to the titles. Don't be afraid to think outside the box. Comb garage sales and talk to the sellers about cutting a deal on books. If your school has an author visit, ask for a signed book donation to your library. The worst that can happen is that he might tell you no. The best that can happen is that you will be able to add free or low-cost materials to your library. Stretch the budget as far as you can.

BUILDING RAPPORT WITH STUDENTS AND TEACHERS

As a 0.5 FTE or less librarian traveling between schools, you may feel particularly challenged trying to build effective rapport with your schools' teachers and students. Hosting a "get to know your library" social is a great way to invite staff into the library while getting to know some of their immediate needs. Ask teachers to put their names in a drawing and offer a certificate for a free book of their choice when you place your book order. Hand out bookmarks with your contact information so teachers feel that you are available to them on a regular basis. Use any publishing program to quickly create and print the bookmarks. If your building has a laminator, use that to make them more durable.

Even though we both work in two schools each day, we are always available to teachers via e-mail to accept materials or collaboration requests. If a book is not available in the district libraries, we offer to use the local public library and pick up and drop off books as a courtesy to teachers. Make a standing offer to teachers so they feel free to bring classes into the library for supplemental lessons. The extra effort in our already busy schedules lets teachers know librarians are available, and it also makes great connections.

Talk to your PTA about having a library open house during an evening event where students and parents can tour the facility, read books together, and network with each other. This is a prime opportunity to connect siblings, especially if students have different last names. Ask parents and students to wear name tags. Talk to parents about volunteering periodically in your library and have a schedule available for sign-ups. Create a short scavenger hunt for the children. When they finish, the prize might be a pencil, bookmark, piece of candy, or any small and inexpensive incentive. Welcome your students daily with a routine greeting; they will quickly remember your name! To make remembering younger student names easy, create name strips. Students bring the name strip to the checkout desk. This makes associating faces and names quick and easy. Offer high-fives as students enter or exit the library. Ask questions about favorite books or characters and encourage students as much as possible. Before long, you will have library "groupies" and lots of students willing to volunteer and saying hello in the halls even though you might not see classes on a daily or weekly basis.

Working in multiple libraries as a less than 1.0 FTE may seem overwhelming, but with great communication, library clerks, organizational skills, and information technology, stress can be greatly reduced. With great technology, it takes less time to manage schedules and tasks and leaves more time for finding creative ways to manage small budgets, seek out library materials, and build solid rapport with teachers and students.

19

MANAGEMENT TIPS FOR MERGING MULTIPLE SERVICE POINTS

Colleen S. Harris

IN THE span of a summer, the North Carolina State University Libraries' access and delivery services department merged two major services, the Media and Microform Center and the Technology Lending Program, into the functions of the main circulation desk. This chapter addresses management tips for planning and implementing service mergers given this experience.

The North Carolina State University Libraries decided to close the Media and Microform Center (MMC), a library service point that was staffed by 2.5 FTE and held all of the library's media collection in microfilm, microfiche, DVD, VHS, and CD formats. Given that the MMC was heavily used by certain academic departments and was responsible for placing media items on reserve for faculty members, the Libraries were highly cognizant that this change would have an effect on our users. In addition to merging the MMC into the main circulation desk services, the Libraries decided to shift the technology device lending service from the library's Learning Commons (under the research and instructional services department) to the main circulation desk, consolidating transactional interactions for a more convenient "one-stop shop" experience for users. The technology collection consisted of laptops (PC, Macbook, Macbook Pro, and MacAir), digital cameras, digital voice recorders, e-book readers, scientific calculators, handheld and dash-mount GPS units, and more. This merger experience has given the NCSU Libraries' access and delivery services department a unique perspective on merging multiple service points, from which I can draw the following tips.

STAKEHOLDER INPUT IS KEY

Who will be most affected by the merge? Include them. We included the most heavily impacted library departments, library administrators, faculty from across the university, and students in the various surveys, committees, and working groups planning for the service mergers. This is also a great way for you to show that you value your stakeholders' input, showcase working collaboratively, and negotiate for the best outcomes. Your users and staff are much less likely to take offense at any boutique services lost in the merge since they were part of the group assessing and coming to the conclusion that the desired service was no longer feasible.

CHANGE IS A CHANCE TO CHALLENGE YOUR STAFF

How often do your staff get to take charge of change in their workplace? Usually the answer is "not often enough." The upcoming merge is a chance for your staff to show off their expertise as they cross-train each other and provides a learning opportunity that expands their skills, makes their job more complex, and encourages them to work together as a team. In access and delivery services, we found that cross-training staff to provide multiple services increased morale as people expanded their skill sets, became engaged in more technical work, and worked together to address and prepare for the upcoming service changes.

MAP PROCESSES, BUILD EFFICIENCIES

Detailed examination of workflows gives you an opportunity to discover where you have unnecessary duplication of effort, overly complicated processes and procedures, outdated policies, or workflows that may be convenient for staff but hamper (or delay) service to the user. An example from our experience with closing the MMC. On the face of it, absorbing the MMC seemed a simple collection shift. However, once staff and administrators started mapping work processes, it became obvious that there were services we would have to absorb and adapt that would include significant documentation and retraining. Processing media reserves, scheduling film viewings and theater reservations, and serving as the service point for our consortium's media lending were processes and policies that required considerable staff training, collaboration, and coordination to redistribute.

COMMUNICATE CLEARLY

For access services to relabel items properly, create space for the media and technology collections behind the main circulation desk and at the satellite shelving facility, develop training manuals, and request timely changes in the catalog, communication was key. Clear communication was also necessary to prepare users for the upcoming changes before the merges, and to redirect them from the old system once the merge was complete. Remember the importance of clear and concise e-mail and verbal communication, verification that all parties are on the same page when decisions are made, and appropriate signage and announcements for your users.

DOCUMENT DECISION MAKING

With all of the meetings and inputs from various stakeholders, it is a good idea to make note somewhere (department wiki, minutes, etc.) of the reasons certain decisions are reached. Think about it as part of the library's institutional history—when things change in the future (as they inevitably will), you do not want people to have to guess why those decisions were made. Record which factors were crucial when you were weighing decisions and you will save future folks from having to reinvent the wheel. Developers document their software, legislators maintain a history of their decisions, and we should do no less as we plan the course of action for our libraries.

TIME TRAINING IS TIME WELL SPENT

Developing training manuals (for both reserves and technology lending), training staff, and developing and maintaining a new schedule and communication system for our incoming student workers were all essential to our success in merging our service points. Staff appreciated that they were well prepared before the transition was completed, our users appreciated that the service switch was nearly seamless, and the time investment was well worth it. Be sure that your people have the resources they need to be successful in the new endeavor.

HAND OVER THE REINS

One of the big tricks to a merge is defining an end point. Without this, policies, procedures, and processes can languish in an in-between state, with people from various departments taking responsibility for various pieces of the merged service and no one having real accountability for the actual implementation of the merge. The key is to have a done-date—that date on which the merged service is officially handed off and everyone moves on.

MAKE DECISIONS, DON'T MARRY THEM

Remember that nothing is set in stone. If something about your service merge is not working as well as you had hoped, examine the reasons behind the failure and change as necessary. For us, it quickly became obvious that housing the teaching media collection and the reserves media collections behind the circulation desk, but leaving the regular circulating media collection in a different wing of the library, was confusing and frustrating for users, particularly as they encountered the new service model. We solved this issue by placing all media in the library behind the circulation desk, but it is likely that we will revisit this in the future as we find a good way to differentiate between the collections. For now, we have sufficient space behind our desk to accommodate these collections, and our users are happier. This sort of flexibility and response to user concern on the part of the library demonstrates commitment to service—as opposed to commitment to the convenience of workflow over user experience.

Almost a year after our service merges, they have been a resounding success. The MMC has been closed, the collection has been reallocated, and reserves processing and consortial media lending now run through the access and delivery staff. Technology lending has also been a resounding success, and we have increased our technology holdings to meet the constant demand and reduce wait-list time for users. Our desk traffic has increased tremendously, and staff members are lively and engaged at our always-bustling main service desk. We wish you similar success in your own service merges.

20

SUPERSTARZ: AN EXPERIENCE IN GRANT PROJECT MANAGEMENT

Vera Gubnitskaia

THE ORANGE County (Florida) Library System received an LSTA grant for $107,704 to conduct SuperStarz: Skill Building for Underserved Children weekly classes at seven Orlando community centers' afterschool programs utilizing mobile computer labs and promoting library resources. Our target group included children in grades three to five as well as their parents and center counselors and managers. The project ran from October 1, 2008, through September 30, 2009. Planning and preparation took place in the first quarter and classes started in January 2009.

GOALS

The project's immediate goals were to provide access to library resources to children who had difficulty accessing them and to introduce to them tools for building school skills and practice test-taking. Mid-range goals included providing the children and caregivers tools that they could use after the grant period was over and promoting library card registration and library resources. In the long term, we hoped to establish and strengthen the library system's relationship with the City of Orlando Families, Parks and Recreation Department and with the community centers, allowing us to tap into the population pool served by the community centers and to help all partner organizations make the use of their funds more efficient.

PLANNING PERIOD

The project manager met with the administration of the Families, Parks and Recreation Department to discuss the details of the project and with each center's manager and other staff to discuss the program and finalize the schedule. Additionally, the manager met with the Orange County Library System's department and division heads participating in the project. Separate action plans with due dates were developed to ensure that preplanning objectives were met in a timely manner. The team of librarians was then selected to serve as instructors and content developers, and additional library staff were identified to serve as support personnel during classes.

Supplies featuring the SuperStarz logo were purchased to help students keep class materials, handouts, and completed work organized. Library materials (books and DVDs), computer hardware and software, and wireless technology were purchased in the first quarter. Equipment was configured and necessary software installed. Mobile labs were installed at three library locations.

MARKETING AND PUBLICITY

The community relations department and project manager developed and implemented the marketing plan. Activities included

- developing the project logo
- placing ads in the local newspaper
- printing and distributing flyers and bookmarks to market the program
- attending the events at the community centers to talk to the attendees and inform them about the program
- submitting information to the City of Orlando and Orange County Public Schools

TEAM TRAINING AND SUPPORT

A team of managers and librarians developed the curriculum and lesson plans and wrote scripts based on subjects studied in grades three to five. Class support and promotional materials were developed, including database user guides and bookmarks, library registration cards, and informational posters. The project manager developed a wiki at superstarz.pbwiki.com to facilitate communication and resource sharing among SuperStarz team members. The wiki was populated with lesson plans, PowerPoint presentations, information about each community center, and instructors' notes and feedback.

Several team meetings and training sessions were held for library instructors and managers:

- introductory meeting to present the project and its goals and objectives
- technology training session at which a trainer demonstrated equipment to be used
- curriculum training session for team instructors
- online classes for instructors presented by database vendors, such as World Book and Tutor.com
- training sessions for instructors on Adobe Connect and Adobe Presenter to learn how to develop virtual classes
- mid-project team meetings to facilitate discussion and exchange ideas

Five web-based tutorials were developed by team instructors on the subjects presented during "live" classes, and a SuperStarz page was created on the Orange County Library System homework-help website.

We distributed entry and exit surveys to children and their parents at community centers, collected and analyzed the resulting data, and created reports using FCAT Explorer to monitor the number of FCAT explorer sessions, subjects practiced, and students' progress. Transcripts of tutor.com sessions were supplied by the vendor to evaluate the success of the sessions.

FEEDBACK AND STEPS FOR IMPROVEMENT

One of the goals of the grant was to provide library access to the population that had difficulty accessing it before. We understood that some kids might not have library cards and therefore would not be able to access the databases. To address the issue, a special library account was created that allowed instructors to sign up children to use databases during the classes. Instructors emphasized to their audience that they should have their own cards if they wanted to use the same products outside the SuperStarz classroom. Instructors distributed card registration forms to kids that their parents could fill out at home. After they brought registrations to the class, the library issued cards and mailed them to students.

To allow statistical analysis of skills development, the project manager created seven "classrooms" on the FCAT Explorer website, with each community center being a class. This allowed the manager to monitor students' progress in FCAT Explorer and make adjustments to the class content.

Instructors reported occasional problems with wireless connection at community centers. To address the issue, the team developed PowerPoint presentations that included screenshots from online products that instructors would usually present in "live" sessions. This allowed instructors to mimic the live session until the connection was restored. Presentations were shared with all instructors through the SuperStarz wiki.

Instructors reported the need for additional activities at the beginning and end of each session; these would allow children to get focused in the beginning and "wind down" at the end of the class. Several puzzles, mazes, and other activities were scanned and posted on the team wiki to use in classes for this purpose.

Librarians used mobile computer labs that carried laptops, LCD projectors, portable screens, and other equipment and supplies. Instructors offered suggestions on making transport of the equipment easier and safer. Additional supplies were purchased or existing library supplies used to address the issue.

After analyzing entry surveys, we found that even children who had library cards did not know how to access and use the library online. Instructors began placing special emphasis on signing kids up for library cards and explaining how they could use library resources from home, school, or a community center. This information was also included in the virtual class recordings.

RESULTS

We completed all three goals set forth at the beginning of the grant period. We introduced school children and their caregivers to library resources that could be accessed remotely, provided them with tools and information they would be able to utilize beyond the program, and strengthened our relationship with the City of Orlando government agencies.

To implement the project, our team developed seventeen lesson plans and recorded five virtual tutorials. The library conducted 177 classes that were attended by 2,128 children, and 602 visitors utilized online classes. Because of budget cuts and subsequent staffing issues, the library was not able to continue regular outreach classes at community centers, but the project continues to benefit the library and community. SuperStarz materials, equipment, and virtual classes are being used during other library activities. We also built a good foundation, developed important partnerships, and gained valuable experience that will be utilized in future projects.

21

UTILIZING RETIRED INDIVIDUALS AS VOLUNTEERS

Ashanti White

RETIREMENT ONCE marked the declining years of a life; it was the time in which a retiree rested. With increased life expectancy and good health, seniors now view retirement as a new period in the journey, one of exploration, learning, and new lifestyles. One factor has remained—senior citizens continue to comprise a large percentage of the public library customers, and many still view the library as a community pillar. Libraries should utilize the enthusiasm and commitment of senior citizens in the community through volunteerism projects that benefit both.

ATTRACTING RETIREES

Volunteerism has proved an integral component of many public library systems, yet administrators, prompted partially by the restraints of some volunteers, have relegated their duties to menial tasks such as sorting and shelving. Such duties are not unimportant, but for library volunteerism to appeal to older customers, who can just as easily find part-time positions elsewhere, some volunteer tasks must be mentally

RETIREMENT BY THE NUMBERS

- One of the 77 million baby boomers reaches age 50 every seven seconds. That is around 11,960 people a day and 4 million a year.
- In 2001, 77 million Americans were 50 and older (28 percent of the population). By 2020, that segment will be 36 percent of the population.
- Nearly 6,000 Americans turn 65 every day, and that figure will jump to 9,000 as the baby boomers age.
- Nearly 35 million Americans were 65 or older in year 2000.[1]

challenging and emotionally rewarding. Unlike teenage or community service candidates, senior citizens bring a special set of skills that can enhance the flow of library duties. Former school teachers and librarians have experience with children, so they can serve as storytime readers, and customer service retirees bring qualities that are necessary in conducting successful surveys. The key to maximizing efforts is thinking innovatively when considering activities that seniors can fulfill.

For example, Libraries for the Future partnered with the Connecticut state library to host the Connecticut Life Options Project, which involved two programs utilizing the skills of older adults to help young children. The Dwight branch of the Hartford Public Library collaborated with a senior center on an intergenerational garden improvement project, and the library in New Haven sponsored the Ben Carson Reading Club, in which older adult volunteers engaged young people in afterschool and family reading activities.[2]

LESS IS MORE

Regardless of the level of volunteer involvement, some training is necessary, especially to inform recruits of library procedures and ethics. Still, we can utilize the expertise and skills of volunteers to reduce the amount of staff time needed. Many public library systems recognize that a major interest for seniors is acquiring basic computer knowledge. Instead of plucking two staff members from regular duties, one librarian can work in conjunction with a volunteer familiar with Internet applications or word processing software. This allows other staff to focus on the overall workflow of the library, allows the training senior to utilize his knowledge, and allows customers to take advantage of germane library programs.

Volunteers can assist in a variety of specialized responsibilities, such as finding requested books, covering books, and providing technical services help in the computer areas, but some may also

STRENGTH IN NUMBERS

In 2009, Fairfax County (Virginia) Public Library volunteers, ages 12–94, donated almost 145,000 hours of work to the library. Many volunteers completed short-term projects, but others have stayed for twenty-five years.[3]

enjoy more leisurely activities. At Camden Public Library, for example, "experienced" volunteers serve as chaperones for the young adult and juvenile programs, in which they man different activity stations for the events. They may also "babysit" equipment during movie showings to ensure that all goes smoothly. Displays, which are important aspects of in-branch marketing, can serve as a creative outlet for retirees volunteering at the library. These tasks are diminutive but a necessary part of library programs.

Guilford College in Greensboro, North Carolina, was founded by Quakers in 1837. The university's main library, Hege Library, maintains an impressive archival collection on Quakers in the Southeast. Most of the volunteers for the Friends Historical Collection and Archives are volunteers from the retirement community, Friends Home, near the institution. Not only do the volunteers greet guests and assist with basic research, many serve as interviewees for primary research.

Although libraries should be creative in designating tasks to retirees, volunteers are welcome to perform the regular tasks too; shelving DVDs, shelf reading, and emptying book drops are always needed.

IDEAL VOLUNTEERS

Retired volunteers are not simply different from other volunteers because of their age. They bring professionalism and experience in various fields. Additionally, they are unlike their teenage and service-mandated candidates in having an indefinite amount of time to donate to the library. If the library can create mentally stimulating and fulfilling activities for retirees, it can reasonably reap the benefits of their secure status. Moreover, the current zeal that seniors possess about their communities and the libraries (e.g., "In addition to my personal use of the library on a regular basis for recreational reading, the library has served my family well through the years")[4] can greatly contribute to the morale of the employees.

Retired volunteers present a host of opportunities to the libraries in which they work. Experience, expertise, professionalism, and passion are among the reasons that libraries should seek to recruit volunteers within this demographic. The recession can take a negative toll on the institutions, but programs and services to customers do not have to be compromised. By supplying retirees rewarding challenges, libraries, customers, and the retiree volunteers all benefit.

Notes

1. Data from *Federal Registrar* 74, no. 14 (January 23, 2009): 4199–201.
2. Diantha Dow Schull, "A New Look at Lifelong Access," *American Libraries,* September 2005:43.
3. Library Volunteer Program. Fairfax County Public Library, www.fairfaxcounty.gov/ library/volunteer/.
4. Hancock County Library System, *Library News*, 2008, www.hatt.ent.sirsi.net/custom/ web/content/mylibrary.doc.

22

WEEDING AS AFFECTIVE RESPONSE, OR "I JUST CAN'T THROW THIS OUT!"

Barbara Fiehn and Roxanne Myers Spencer

Barbara Fiehn: Years of weeding collections have honed my deselection skills. Recently I volunteered to assist in weeding a children's collection in an academic library. My weeding partners were knowledgeable but angst-filled professionals. Finding a balance between our views on weeding has been an ongoing, enjoyable learning experience.

Roxanne Spencer: I wanted to explore this topic because I am a reluctant weeder. I am one of those librarians Diane Young challenged when she said, "Raise your hand if you can't face weeding."[1] I fit a few of the weeding personalities we jocularly identify below.

THE DEBATE to weed or not to weed can be traced to the 1890s in the controversy over the Quincy Plan for weeding the Crane Memorial Public Library in Quincy, Massachusetts.[2] The ensuing debate between the weeders and the preservationists continues today.

Every librarian knows the basics of weeding, but applying that knowledge can be difficult. The non-weeder and new weeder must understand and overcome any mental inhibitors. For some, withdrawing a book stimulates an emotional response similar to grieving. In "Crying Over Spilt Milk," Gail Dickinson presents a concise overview for solo librarians and compares keeping outdated materials to keeping outdated milk. She also outlines a three-step weeding process that takes fifteen minutes per week for small libraries.[3]

The analysis and evaluation of any library collection requires time, planning, and the involvement of all staff. In public or academic settings, staff or student assistants should be trained to review and withdraw materials. School librarians often do not have additional staff. Utilizing and training teachers, students, and PTO volunteers involve the community and gives participants a sense of ownership.[4]

WEEDING MODELS

The CREW method, along with its MUSTIE (or MUSTY) relatives, is used in public or school libraries.[5] In academic libraries, collection evaluation often follows the Research Libraries Group (RLG) or WLN Conspectus methods.[6] Whichever guidelines are used, consideration must be given to what will be weeded, the extent of weeding, the weeding criteria, and quality control. Preparation and adherence to requirements are essential for training library staff to weed effectively. Without a clear understanding of the library's collection needs, the weeding personalities we describe below can skew results.

WEEDING PERSONALITIES

The spectrum of librarians as weeders extends from those who see the process as a challenge, leading to a lean and marketable collection, to those who respond with horror to the thought of weeding. All librarians have a weeding personality. The following is a light-hearted look at some familiar types:

Weed-whacker. Goes through the collection like it's hay-mowing time, leaving shelves as bare as a stubbled field.

One-in/one-out. Lean BMI (book mass index); small space, budget, collection.

Beauty contest weeder. Always judges a book by its cover.

Plays favorites. Weeds everything except their favorite authors, illustrators, titles, subjects.

Award-verification weeder. Keeps every award, honor, notable, starred-review title ever published.

Scientific weeder. Uses lengthy charts, tables, and citation analysis from multiple weeding studies.

Nostalgic weeder. Breakin' up is hard to do.

Worrywart weeder. What if somebody wants . . . ?

Subversive. Appears to weed but reshelves titles others have discarded.

Retriever/dumpster diver. Reclaims withdrawn titles in the name of "preservation" and fear of the public's negative perception.

Packrat. Does not willingly weed anything, ever. Period.

NEGATIVE RESPONSES

Library staff may have issues about withdrawing library materials beyond those implied by the personalities above. Although the profession agrees on general standards for weeding, many librarians still question weeding their own collections. Common negative responses to the process include these:

- Someone may need this someday.
- The out-of-date stuff is minimal; there is still relevant information.
- Finding selection errors is demoralizing.

- No time: there are too many other things to do.
- If we weed everything that is out of date, we will not have anything on some subjects.
- Expensive items should not be weeded; it is a waste of taxpayers' money.
- We cannot remove classic titles, even if no one has looked at them in forty years.
- Donations will be missed if weeded.
- The public will react negatively if they see too many discarded items.
- First editions may be valuable some day and must be retained.
- It sells for $____ on Alibris. We can't throw it away!
- Processing and disposal of deselected material are cumbersome and time consuming.

Rules of thumb for severe weeding:

- If in doubt—throw it out!
- Not checked out—get it out!

ACTUALIZATION

Few librarians find the weeding process to be intrinsically reinforcing. Most acknowledge it as necessary and important. Many also exhibit strong avoidance behaviors in approaching weeding. Building reinforcements into the process assists forward movement (chocolate works). Targeted praise and encouragement build conscious commitment to the weeding project. A variety of different considerations are relevant to getting non-weeders to weed, and several different tactics help:

- Get the administrators to require action.
- Weed a little at a time to make the task less overwhelming.
- Weed the most obvious things first.
- Commit to a weeding schedule and be held accountable.
- Reward yourself and others with each incremental goal achieved.
- Set specific goals and parameters (e.g., circulation statistics, age, condition, outdated information) and use them.
- Use a buddy system for support.
- Get help from nonlibrarian subject specialists.
- Share the worst of the weeding projects. It sets the stage for some good laughs.

WEEDING AFFIRMATIONS

Sometimes a little "self-prepping" may be useful for librarians to take on the weeding challenge. Remind weeders of the long-term, positive outcomes of the process with encouraging thoughts, like these:

- "I am helping to make our library collection more user-friendly and usable."
- "The shelves are much easier to browse when weeded."
- "I'll have more room to display new titles."
- "I can't believe this book was on the shelf. This section needed weeding."
- "Patrons have noticed the 'spruced-up' look of the library."
- "I did it!" "We did it!"
- "I'm glad it is done. It really wasn't so bad."

Help reluctant weeders with thoughtful planning, incentives, and adherence to professional standards. Some librarians still feel guilty about weeding, despite the theoretical knowledge and reinforcement that pruning a collection is good. These librarians, by disposition, should not weed. Recognize that converting non-weeders to the cause is neither likely nor the ultimate goal. The goal is to maintain a viable, vital, resilient collection for our patrons.

Notes

1. Diane J. Young, "Get to Effective Weeding," *Library Journal* 134, no. 19 (2009): 36.
2. Juris Dilevko and Lisa Gottlieb, "Weed to Achieve: A Fundamental Part of the Public Library Mission?" *Library Collections, Acquisitions, and Technical Services* 27 (2003): 73–96.
3. Gail Dickinson, "Crying Over Spilt Milk," *Library Media Connection*, April/May 2005, www.linworth.com/pdf/lmc/reviews_and_articles/featured_articles/Dickinson_April_May2005.pdf.
4. Brian Mathews, "Next Steps: Weeding Grows the Garden," *American Libraries*, April 16, 2010, www.americanlibrariesmagazine.org/columns/next-steps/weeding-grows-garden.
5. Texas State Library and Archives Commission, *CREW: A Weeding Manual for Modern Libraries*, 2008, www.tsl.state.tx.us/ld/pubs/crew/crewmethod08.pdf.
6. Library of Congress, Cataloging and Acquisitions: Collecting Levels [RLG], www.loc.gov/acq/devpol/cpc.html. Georgine Olson, "WLN Conspectus: An Introduction," *Collection Building* 13, nos. 2/3 (1994): 29.

PART III
Information Technology

23

FACEBOOK FOR STUDENT ASSISTANTS

Susan Jennings and Ken Johnson

ACCORDING TO recent data from the Pew Internet and American Life Project, 72 percent of online adults age 18–29 use social networking sites, and 71 percent of those use Facebook as their social network of choice. Furthermore, over 93 percent of young adults own a cell phone.[1] With these facts in mind, the Student Training Taskforce at Appalachian State University's Belk Library and Information Commons decided to embrace the trend and use this technology as a practical means of communication with students.

Belk Library employs more than one hundred student assistants who work in various departments and on different shifts during the library's 112 weekly service hours. Their physical and chronological dispersion makes it difficult for supervisors to communicate efficiently with them. In early 2008, the Student Training Taskforce created a Facebook group to address this problem. This case study explains how we implemented the group and lessons we learned from our experience.

WHY FACEBOOK?

Facebook allows communication via any Internet-ready device and through any computer platform. All that is needed is an Internet connection, whether through a handheld device or through traditional computer access. E-mail offers the same benefit, but research like the Pew study reflects, and our own internal polling suggests, that students often stay connected through Facebook while they do other things, making Facebook communication instantaneous. Thus, it just made sense for our library to try Facebook as a tool to communicate with our student workers.

PRELIMINARY USES

One of our service desk managers first adopted Facebook to communicate with her students. With Facebook, the desk manager experienced a faster response to open shifts, questions, and announcements than she had seen via the traditional e-mail communication methods. Coincidentally, technological problems hampered our campuswide e-mail system around that time, which delayed traditional communication efforts. Creating a private Facebook group as the primary means of supervisor-to-student communication simply worked better than e-mail, and the students really liked it. Students were now able to communicate with us on a traditional computer, cell phone, or other handheld device.

Building on the desk manager's early success, the Student Training Taskforce conducted a poll of all library student assistants and supervisors to ascertain who might be using Facebook already. Student responses showed that around 70 percent already had a Facebook account and that most used Facebook daily. Our results are similar to the Pew study findings. In contrast, most supervisors did not have their own Facebook account but were open to the possibility.

Convinced by the apparent enthusiasm for the Facebook project, the Student Training Taskforce created a Facebook group titled the "ASU Student Training Page." The taskforce sent e-mail invitations to all student assistants, and seventy-one students accepted the invitation to join. The taskforce was encouraged by the seventy-one members, though it fell short of 100 percent participation.

CREATION AND IMPLEMENTATION OF THE FACEBOOK GROUP LIBRARY-WIDE

Membership in the student training group was by invitation only, since some of the information posted might be of a private nature. We gave student supervisors administrative privileges to the site that enabled them to upload videos and pictures and post messages to members of the group. We granted students "wall" privileges in order to communicate with supervisors and each other. Although all supervisors who participated had administrative privileges to the group, in reality only a few supervisors posted new information on a regular basis.

Although the initial focus was to announce training opportunities and events, supervisors have used this site to advertise for student help among the already trained cadre of students, thereby further supporting a library-wide cross-training initiative. This opportunity provided variety for student assistants and gave them the chance to cultivate skills beyond those learned working in their primary department. With Facebook, our communications reached our students quickly and student response time improved.

OBSERVATIONS IN SUPPORT OF OUR EFFORTS

Use of the ASU Student Training Page has produced many positive outcomes. We have observed that the Facebook group has created

- opportunities for cross-training in other areas of the library, resulting in more well-rounded student assistants
- a sense of community and increased communication among student assistants and supervisors, lessening the sense of isolation felt in a facility so large
- one site for ongoing training through posts of tips and tricks from knowledgeable staff and librarians in various areas
- a demonstrated sense of ownership, pride, and commitment from the student assistants
- a ready-made focus group with which to vet new ideas and services

LESSONS LEARNED

We are pleased with the improvements in student communication using the ASU Student Training Group. For others interested in this type of initiative, here are some of the lessons we learned:

- Create buy-in from student supervisors and get them involved in the process early.
- Take the lead: Anyone with an Internet connection and a Facebook account can create a group. Leaders must dedicate the time, generate the buzz, and commit to the project for the duration.
- Calm fears about social networking in general, especially for those not accustomed to the technology. Educating students and supervisors about how Facebook works and how to set privacy settings allays most fears and preconceptions.
- Keep the group relevant. Many of our student assistants are eager to earn more money and learn new skills. By adopting the Facebook group as the primary means of communication, the students continue to find out about openings and the latest training opportunities available.
- Garner support from library administrators from the beginning. Early support from administrators helped us overcome initial resistance.
- Build a core group of dedicated super-users. Even one leader, no matter how dynamic, cannot manage the site alone. Enlist the assistance of others to post and provide feedback.
- Avoid competing avenues of communication to lessen confusion and information overload. We use Facebook as our official library communication tool for student assistants and send very little e-mail.
- Promote the group to new hires and use their enthusiasm to grow support.
- Monitor student assistant communication trends and do not be afraid to adopt a new technological tool. At some point, even Facebook may become obsolete.

After two years, Belk Library's ASU Student Training group is still a successful yet simple portal for scheduling, networking, announcements, and training. As technology and students change, the Student Training Taskforce will continue to investigate new and better ways to foster communication with our student assistants. For now, through the use of Facebook, the student assistants and supervisors have come together and are truly on the same page.

Note

1. Amanda Lenhart, Kristen Purcell, Aaron Smith, and Kathryn Zickuhr, "Social Media and Mobile Internet Use among Teens and Young Adults," *Pew Internet and American Life Project*, February 2010, http://pewresearch.org/pubs/1484/social-media-mobile -internet-use-teens-millennials-fewer-blog.

24

IMPROVING COMMUNICATION WITH BLOGS

Alice B. Ruleman

THE CONCEPT of blogs in the library has generated a good bit of interest in the past few years. Most of the information is about using *external* blogs to provide information and generate discussion among patrons, but blogs can also be very useful for internal communication. This chapter challenges you to look beyond your preconceived notions about blogs to think about new ways they can benefit your library.

CHARACTERISTICS OF BLOGS

Blogs have certain characteristics that set them apart from other kinds of Web 2.0 technology. Public blogs are usually the responsibility of one person and the style is informal. Blog posts appear in reverse chronological order. Although readers can make comments on the posts, the software does not permit them to edit the original posts. Many blogs are searchable, but the content is ephemeral as new posts are added and older posts are pushed farther down the list. Blogs are good tools for dialog, discussion, and brainstorming.

HOW TO CHOOSE BLOG SOFTWARE

Before selecting blogging software, you need to know what features are available and which ones you need. What are the system requirements? What about data storage, anti-spam, and user access? Weblog Matrix (www.weblogmatrix.org) can be used to compare characteristics of almost thirty blogs.

Darlene Fichter suggests considering these features:[1]

Archives. Are older posts stored or do they disappear?

Search. A search function turns a blog into a searchable databank.

Categories. Bloggers usually write about multiple, distinct topics. Users benefit if the topics can be divided into searchable categories.

Design/appearance. Most blog software provides a gallery of templates. Some let you create your own.

Plug-ins. Many blog programs offer plug-ins to give more control and functionality. For example, the optional WordPress plug-in "Get Recent Comments" displays current comments in the sidebar of your blog according to the criteria you set up.

Community tools. These tools control who can see it and who can leave comments.

BLOG USES IN LIBRARIES

Most of us are familiar with public blogs on the Internet, which share information about everything from what the kids and pets did today to philosophical musing and political commentary. In libraries, blogs can be used by the institution or groups on work-related topics. Here are some possible uses.

Director's blog. A blog is a good medium for library and department heads to keep the staff informed about changes, events, and so forth. A recent e-mail communication from the dean at the University of Central Missouri included an update on the long awaited construction of a café in the library. Replacing the e-mail with a blog would be a good mechanism to encourage questions and discussion about topics that matter to the staff.

Staff blog. Tarleton State University (Texas) uses Blogger for the staff to cover helpful information that does not need to be in their wiki. For instance, a cataloging librarian posted information about a change in the item types on theses and dissertations that simplified searching for them in the OPAC. A staff blog can include links to articles, questions, opinions, or even fun things. Blogger was also the choice at Lewis-Clark State College (Idaho) for the reference desk and circulation staff blogs. Although the circulation blog has been well received by the staff and student workers, the reference blog is not used as frequently.

SOME BLOG APPLICATIONS

- *Typepad*
- *Blogger*
- *WordPress*
- *B2evolution*
- *MovableType*
- *GeekLog*
- *BlogCloud*
- *Loudblog*
- *Cakewalk Blogs*
- *Nucleus CMS*
- *WikiBlog*

Technical information. When the Allen Memorial Library at the University of Hartford (Connecticut) migrated from Voyager to Koha, a blog was set up to inform the staff about the process. Once Koha was in place, the blog continued to be used to give updates on problems, new developments, and planned improvements.

Reference desk blog. WordPress was selected by Bowling Green State University (Ohio) for its RefBlog, and it has proved to be an effective communication tool. Reading the current postings is part of the routine for everyone when their desk shift begins. Changes in procedures, general library information, electronic resources updates, problem reports, assignments or tasks for students, and tips on recent tricky reference questions are posted. Reference services on Grant MacEwan University's (Alberta) campuses use DRUPAL. Information specific to one campus (e.g., the copier is not working) is restricted to that campus, but other information is shared with all.

IF YOU BUILD IT, WILL THEY COME?

As with any new program, it can take time for blogs to catch on. At Cisco Systems, Jere King, vice president of marketing, has emerged as one of the most popular bloggers in the company. She shared the following tips for successful blogs, which libraries can adapt.[2]

- Maintain a consistent publication schedule. If people expect to see something new, they are more likely to check the blog regularly. Let everyone know when new information is added.
- Give your readers something to comment on or interact with.
- Readers expect a quick response to their posts. In library departments, staff can share responsibility for monitoring and responding to the blog.
- Create an online "watering hole" to draw them in and encourage discussion.
- Make it worthwhile. We are all busy and do not have time for boring information that is not pertinent.

TO BLOG OR TO WIKI? THAT IS THE QUESTION

Blogs and wikis both provide excellent means of interacting and communicating with other people. Although there are perceived and real differences between the two kinds of software, many times they can be used interchangeably. Academic libraries have successfully used blogs, wikis, and course management systems (e.g., Blackboard for student worker communication using the same basic content). Make your decision based on your project's specific needs.

BLOGS VERSUS WIKIS

Order of posts. Blogs posts are in order with the most recent at the top. Wiki discussion posts are reversed, with the newest response at the bottom. Scrolling can became an issue with a long discussion.

Appearance. Wikis generally have a simple format with the option to change background color and font. The focus is on the content. Blogs are more likely to have themes and templates to select, and many allow users to create their own personalized look and branding. How important is the appearance?

Editing documents. Wikis are designed for collaborative editing, but blogs usually restrict editing to the administrator. If editing documents is a major function of the application, a wiki is a better choice.

Several years ago, Bob Doyle stated that "novel uses of blogs and wikis are rampant."[3] Today, you can still be creative. This chapter mentions a few uses in libraries, but you are not limited to these ideas. If you think your committee, team, or library could benefit from a blog, don't be afraid to try something new.

Notes

1. Darlene Fichter, "Why and How to Use Blogs to Promote Your Library's Services," *Marketing Library Services* 19, no. 6 (2003): 1–4, www.infotoday.com/mls/nov03/ fichter.shtml.
2. Krishna Sanker and Susan A. Bouchard, "Web 2.0 @ Cisco: The Evolution," May 4, 2009, www.ciscopress.com/articles/printerfriendly.asp?p=1336793.
3. Bob Doyle, "When to Wiki, When to Blog," *Econtent Magazine*, July 11, 2006, www .econtentmag.com/Articles/Column/I-Column-Like-I-CM/When-to-Wiki-When-to -Blog-16900.htm.

25

IMPROVING PRODUCTIVITY WITH GOOGLE APPS

Suzann Holland

YOU MAY already use Gmail or other Google services in your personal life, but the Google Apps suite is a great set of tools to manage the many different types of tasks that a library administrator is responsible for. Once you are comfortable with the interface, you may be quickly tempted to leave Outlook behind. Should you choose to do so, the suggestions in this chapter can help you improve your productivity dramatically.

GOOGLE VIA FORWARD

If you are part of a large organization, you may already have an e-mail/calendaring system in place. If you cannot choose your e-mail provider, use Google Apps anyway, using the following steps:

1. Choose a domain name. Perhaps your name is available, as in First nameLastname.com.

2. Set up Google Apps account mapped to the domain name.

3. Create an e-mail address. Remember, each e-mail address is considered a user and costs $50 a year. Consider Work@FirstnameLastname.com or Firstname@FirstnameLastname.com.

4. Forward your work e-mail (direct and any others you are responsible for checking) to the newly created e-mail address.

5. Under Settings, add your work e-mail account. This enables you to send mail using that address. Make it the default.

6. Verify that the setup is correct by sending some test e-mail to and from your work e-mail account through the Google Apps interface.

YOU GET WHAT YOU PAY FOR

You will want to use the paid version of Google Apps for two reasons: it is customizable for your domain, and you receive better technical support. Google guarantees 99.9 percent uptime for their Premier Apps customers, in addition to 25 GB of e-mail storage space. The Google Apps Premier edition is $50 per year, per user.

A text expansion program does even more to improve your productivity with Google Apps. Text expansion programs allow you to create abbreviations for longer text snippets or even whole paragraphs. When you type the abbreviation, the program automatically expands it to the corresponding longer phrase. Consider TextExpander for Mac ($29.95 at www.smileonmymac.com) and Texter for Windows (free at code section of www.lifehacker.com).

Use your text expansion program to facilitate the setup of certain helpful Google Mail filters. For example, create a keyboard shortcut for "File to @Waiting" and insert it at the bottom of e-mail that involves something you have delegated or need an answer on before you can move to the next action. Set up a filter to recognize "File to @Waiting" in outgoing e-mail and label those messages with a "Waiting" designation. To check to see if you need to follow up on anything, just hit the "Waiting" label and you will see a list of all items you are waiting on.

Other helpful labels may include "Logins & Licenses" (a great way to track software registration numbers and log-in credentials not often used), a "Task" label to track simple to-dos you e-mail to yourself, and a "Personal" label to ensure that e-mail that is not work related can be quickly identified and dealt with differently. Use your imagination and create labels that fit your ways of working.

STAFF DELEGATION

Use Google Calendar to quickly track who has been assigned to a particular task and when the task is due to be completed. Begin by creating a separate calendar (Google Calendar allows you to create multiple calendars that you can show or hide with a single click) titled "Staff Deadlines." When you assign a task, create an all-day event named with the staff member's initials and the task. For example, if you assign John Cooper to submit a department budget by March 5, your entry into the Staff Deadline calendar might read "JC—Dept Budget." Assigned more than one person to work on a task jointly? Add an extra set of initials before the hyphen. Conversely, if you assign the same task to be separately completed by more than one person, create a separate event for each person.

In the days leading up to the March 5 deadline, you will see the notation on your calendar and remember to expect the task to be completed. Once John turns in his budget report, simply click on the calendar item and delete it. Has the due date come and gone? If you set up a new standard for immediate follow-up, staff members know that you are serious about due dates and will likely let you know in advance if they run into obstacles that might delay completion.

STAFF SCHEDULING

Google Calendar does not work for actually constructing the schedule itself (unless you have a very small staff), but it is fabulous for tracking schedule requests. Each separate Google Calendar within a single account may be assigned a private URL. The URL for the Schedule Requests calendar can be shared with employees for personal use and bookmarked on staff computers for quick access.

An employee's request for a week's worth of vacation can be easily noted as "John VAC" with a block that can be stretched for whatever days are involved. Other notes, such as "John APT 4pm" and "John off EVE" quickly convey the necessary information.

Require that all schedule requests be submitted via e-mail. This provides a record of the request as submitted in the event of later questions. When you approve a schedule request and add it to the calendar, hit reply and insert a standard message, such as "Approved and posted! Please verify that the online approval calendar is correct," using the text expansion program. Set up a filter to recognize that message, and label your replies with the designation "Schedule." This makes tracking down an old request for verification especially simple.

COLLECTION DEVELOPMENT

Utilize Google Calendar to help manage any materials selection areas you have. Create all-day, repeating events in Google Calendar to ensure that important tasks are attended to on a regular basis. Some suggestions:

- Add a repeating event for May to get a copy of the local high school yearbook.
- Designate certain times of the year to review particular collection areas. In Dewey-classified libraries, take a Dewey class in each of ten months. Skip two months of your choice—perhaps December for the holidays and June for the end of the fiscal year.

- Keep track of serial books such as price guides, almanacs, and test preparation guides.
- Add a repeating event for December to get tax preparation titles and ensure that forms are in stock.
- For media collections, consider how many items you would ideally purchase in a given time period. For example, if you want to add five Blu-rays each month, add a repeating event to "Order 5 Blu-rays."

Many e-mail and calendar systems can be adapted to help boost your productivity. The suggestions presented here are tailored to the Google Apps suite because of my experience with its features and its flexibility. Whatever you use to track your library management tasks, let the system do the recall for you. Carefully consider the questions *who*, *what*, *when*, and *how often*. Automate your task-based actions so that you can quit thinking about them. You will find additional energy to devote to the most skilled and rewarding duties of your position.

26

PARTNERING WITH INFORMATION TECHNOLOGY AT THE REFERENCE DESK: A MODEL FOR SUCCESS

Jeffrey A. Franks

FOR THE past several decades constantly changing technologies have driven innovations in teaching, scholarly research, and communication. Academic librarians have embraced these innovations and incorporated them into daily practice through hard work and ingenuity. In recent years the pace of change and innovation has become continuous. Students now need and expect to receive technical support and reference service simultaneously. Over a relatively short period of time information technology and the ability to locate and use scholarly information have become inextricably bound together. In addition to "Can you help me find books on global warming?" we now routinely hear "Can you help me set up my laptop for the wireless network?" and "I can't open the file my professor sent in an e-mail; can you help?" These examples represent but a small fraction of the growing number of technical queries that users now present at reference desks. Some reference librarians have added new skill sets to their traditional reference arsenal; many others have come to rely on some degree of assistance from campus IT units.

BUILDING A STRONG PARTNERSHIP WITH INFORMATION TECHNOLOGY

The University of Akron Libraries (UL) have a long tradition of innovative partnering with the university's Information Technology Services (ITS). Over a decade ago the two campus units worked together to pioneer a campuswide wireless laptop program. ITS also established a branch of its Technology Learning Support Center at Bierce Library, one of three campus libraries and the main undergraduate library. Though not physically near the reference desk, the presence of the Support Center in the main library facilitated the resolution of the most common IT issues for users.

One could argue that the ultimate incarnation of the reference/IT partnership is the learning commons, where a variety of services are provided in one location. In recent years, the UL and ITS have worked with other campus units to develop a service model for a learning commons to be constructed in Bierce. During the learning commons planning process, both units gained a shared understanding of how the services of each could be enhanced by the presence of the other. Ultimately, whatever the method, academic library users need IT assistance, and they need it now.

WHY WAIT?

All worthwhile efforts take time. Designing, constructing, and equipping a learning commons is under way but will take months to complete. In the meantime, why should students, faculty, and staff, or for that matter reference and IT service providers, wait? The Bierce Library reference department decided to initiate the new model of seamless reference and IT service in advance of the learning commons. The head of reference and the manager of the Learning Technology Support Center, together with key staff, designed a program, and the new service model was officially implemented at the start of the 2009 fall semester.

IDENTIFYING USER EXPECTATIONS

Our program objectives and logistics are based on key aspects of the learning commons concept. One of the most important aspects is that services should be developed around student needs. To identify those needs the reference department logged all questions asked of reference staff for one month and analyzed them to identify the most common IT issues. A recent LibQUAL was also reviewed and Support Center personnel were consulted. The following list reflects the most common technical issues that students presented at the reference desk:

General issues

- network log-in and passwords
- online course registration
- university e-mail
- operating systems (Vista, XP, etc.)

File issues

- recovering corrupted files
- resolving file incompatibility
- opening zipped files
- document conversion (Office 2003 to 2007, Word to PDF, etc.)
- e-mail attachments that do not open or print
- locating missing files

Laptop issues

- wireless network configuration
- network printer configuration
- synchronization problems (wireless network and Ethernet)

Web-based course instruction issues (using Springboard)

- accessing files
- moving files
- locating tutorials
- printing from Springboard

Office 2007 issues

- Word basics
- Excel basics
- PowerPoint basics

CREATING A SEAMLESS SERVICE

To respond quickly and efficiently to the above types of queries, the new model includes a highly trained IT Support Center student assistant working side by side with reference providers at a single service point, the reference desk. This arrangement provides a mechanism for reference personnel to coordinate initial queries quickly and refer technical issues to the IT student assistant. In this way the disconnect that occurs when services are located separately is eliminated and users are provided with a more seamless service.

Which queries do we refer? Reference personnel, especially student assistants or peer helpers, are able to assist users with many basic technical issues. Some issues require additional technical expertise, and there are times when all reference personnel are assisting with reference inquiries. For these reasons the IT student usually fields all but the most basic technical queries.

Another component of the model is visibility. All reference and IT student assistants or peer helpers are clearly identified by brightly colored T-shirts with university logos and the words "Ask Me" on the back. This visibility is essential when peer helpers are away from the service desk performing their roving duties.

DEVELOPING A COMPREHENSIVE TRAINING PROGRAM

The new model includes a comprehensive IT training program for all UL public service staff and student assistants, with particular emphasis on reference peer helpers. The most highly trained IT Support Center students are called "lead technicians." Using the above list of issues as a starting point, these individuals worked closely with the reference department to develop a training program that addresses the most common technical issues relevant to the information and reference process. Reference peer helpers were the first group to be trained. Once their training was completed, training was offered to other UL public service staff and student assistants.

Training is performed by the lead technicians at the Support Center and is flexible enough to be conducted in a one-on-one or small group venue, depending on the specific learning styles of individuals. It is supported by training documents, online tutorials, and a Support Center wiki.[1] New reference students are trained when hired. New students and staff in other departments may receive training from a lead technician on request or, if they prefer, they may be trained by one of their peers who have completed the training. Training objectives include the following:

- Student assistants and staff will be able to provide frontline assistance in using information technology effectively.
- Student assistants and staff will work in an enhanced synergistic fashion with the support desk on the ground floor.

An assessment of training outcomes is a key aspect of the training program and is to include methods to measure the effectiveness of the training program, including post-tests for trainees and user surveys, and mechanisms for providing regular formal and informal feedback to the head of reference services and the manager of technology learning support services.

Most library users do not differentiate between information needs and technology needs when they come to the library to complete their research and assignments. They do not know, nor should they need to know, the difference between a librarian and an IT specialist. Eliminating the confusion and the obstacle of having to go to separate service points for different types of assistance enhances the learning process and contributes to academic success. By forging ahead with this program we have achieved a more seamless, blended service that combines the expertise of reference providers with the special skills of IT personnel at one service location.

Note
1. University of Akron Support Center wiki: http://support.uakron.edu/wiki/index.php/Main_Page.

27

PUTTING MISSING PIECES FROM THE COLLECTION TOGETHER WITH SHAREPOINT

Lorette S. J. Weldon

I HAVE found through the years that communication is key to running a successful collection. The best approach for the communication is to use a tool that many information professionals are familiar with—and that would be social media sites. As a manager of a special collection, I figured out how to design a Microsoft SharePoint site to capture and classify tacit knowledge pertaining to the subject areas of the collection. This "how-to" chapter shows you how to create such a site without coding and how to facilitate measurement of successes or failures through documentation of the quality and quantity of knowledge artifacts.

Through a survey conducted during a ten-day period in July 2009, I gathered data that showed that special collections in the government, nonprofit, for-profit, and academic sectors were using professional learning networks (PLN) without realizing it. The PLN is usually through social media site environments to improve communication channels with staff and customers. PLNs are online communities where you are free to share your research and get feedback from your peers and colleagues. The key is working together. The results of this activity rely on your interpretations of the discussions.[1]

The survey gave the impression that librarians have been using blogs and social networking sites to communicate research findings to their customers. This impression showed that librarians could easily move toward a SharePoint environment.[2] A total of 441 individuals responded to the survey. Individuals in library science used social media sites in the workplace more than individuals in business and education

---

SURVEY RESULTS: USAGE OF SOCIAL MEDIA SITES FOR WORK

Who is using it?	Social media sites used to communicate with/for	Social media sites used the most in the workplace
• Library science, 49%	• Staff/customers, 39%	• LinkedIn, 38%
• Business, 23%	• Research, 27%	• Facebook, 27%
• Education, 18%	• Pleasure, 22%	• Twitter, 22%
• Other, 11%	• Boredom, 12%	• MySpace, 2%
		• Other, 12%

(see Survey Results). The Pew Research Center corroborated the general conclusion, stating that their studies found 52 percent of adults using social networking sites.[3]

WHAT IS SHAREPOINT?

If you are about to install and configure SharePoint on your organization's server, it would be called Microsoft SharePoint 2007 (MOSS for short in the IT world). If you are using a hosted SharePoint site, you could be using Windows SharePoint Services 3.0. SharePoint helps you manage the prime real estate on your organization's server or hosted space. Look at SharePoint as a home improver. It helps you organize the storage space so that you can find all of the knowledge artifacts (see Vocabulary to Know) your organization needs for projects.

VOCABULARY TO KNOW

tacit knowledge: lived experiences, thoughts, ideas

artifacts: tangible objects that define your organization's activities

SharePoint portal: a basic website within your intranet on your server

document management: organization of artifacts

collaboration: sharing experiences and tangible objects with coworkers and contacts that may produce more experiences and tangible objects

---

Out of the box, SharePoint automatically gives you the following rooms (modules) for your house, but you have to figure out which ones you need. You may not need all of these modules in the beginning:

- wikis
- workspaces
- document library
- announcements
- RSS feeds
- e-alerts
- discussion boards

The house shown in figure 1 was designed for an organization of thirty staff members.[4] As you can see, the modules are similar to those components you find on social networking sites like LinkedIn, Facebook, and MySpace. Through these modules, your work environment helps you and your staff perform the following:

- collaborate with each other and with customers
- develop the information in the collection into updatable artifacts

- define workflows more efficiently
- have direct access to the most current version of a document
- access people's reflections on past and current projects in wikis and blogs

Because Microsoft relied on its customers to look for "the familiar" in the online work environment, it placed a wizard tool similar to the ones within Microsoft Office. Microsoft has given its wizard tool a name, SharePoint. Microsoft also gives you a database (MSDE) that SharePoint functions with so that you never have to do "advance" programming for basic functions to be performed.[5]

YOUR LIBRARY'S COMMUNICATION WEBSITE

Figuring out how your collection can deal with tacit knowledge is dependent on your communication culture. SharePoint allows you to share ideas, breaking down those information "silos" and "smokestacks." The ideas you share are experiences and rules of thumb that are not ordinarily written down before, during, or after projects. Explicit knowledge is usually the project report, which typically entails the summary of what your department accomplished for that quarter. This probably includes a description of the customers you helped and the requests you completed. Through SharePoint, you can actually include people's thought processes and feedback.[6]

FIGURE 1

Let's make your communication website (portal) so that you do not lose any more "lived experiences" from your coworkers.

1. Open a new SharePoint site on your server at work. You need permission from the IT department to have this type of power; this is permission for your site only. If you are using a hosting service, such as Apptix, type in the hosting service's website address (www.sharepointsite.com) and create an account.

2. Once the account is created, an e-mail is sent to you so that you can create your site.

3. SharePoint asks you what type of site you want. SharePoint has website templates for you to choose from. This chapter focuses on the knowledge base template, so select it. Other templates suitable for library collections are Document Library and Review and Lending Library (see figure 2).

4. Through a hosted site, SharePoint prompts you for the users of the site. You can enter this by hand. If you have SharePoint on your server, the users for the site come from your exchange server. You may have to talk to your IT department to get clarification, if SharePoint is housed on a server.

FIGURE 2

Template Name	Description	Business Area
Document Library and Review*	Help teams manage the document library including a threaded discussion to provide a feedback.	*Project/Document development*
Knowledge Base*	Enable employees to share knowledge resident within their organization	*Project Tracking/ Elicit ideas from co-workers*
Lending Library*	Help manage the physical assets in an organization's library with check out/in functionality and automated overdue notification.	*Physical or electronic document tracking*

5. Next, SharePoint gives you a basic site (see figure 3). You now have a communication portal for your team, department, library, or library system. It can be customized or kept the way it is. For this chapter, we keep it in the default mode.

6. Click on "Create a Keyword" link on the homepage and enter in the categories for the ideas (tacit knowledge) that your staff will be sharing with each other (see figure 4). The categories can follow the subject areas of your collection.

7. Once you have finished clicking on "New" to add your categories, click on the icon to your left called "Team Web Site." This takes you back to the homepage.

CAN WE TALK?

Your new communication portal displays ideas that are shared for the day, week, or month. Here is how you can open your communication portal for you and your staff:

1. Click on "Write an Article." You and your staff can jot thoughts down that are related to the categories in the box.

2. Select the categories by clicking on the category and then by clicking on the "Add" button. Your selection is moved into the box of selected categories. You can do this with as many of the categories that fit what you will be writing about.

3. Click your mouse in the "Title" box and type in a title for the idea you want to share.

FIGURE 3

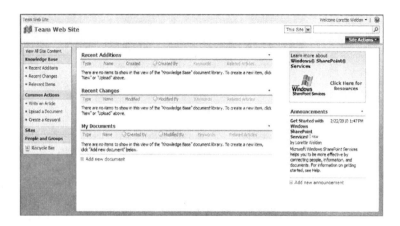

FIGURE 4

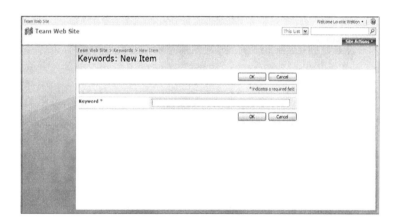

4. Click your mouse in the "Article Content" box. Start typing your thought. SharePoint comes with a basic word processor that allows different fonts and linking to other websites.

5. Scroll to the bottom of the page and you can make a relationship with your thought to anyone else's typed thought (see figure 5).[7]

6. To add a document that you would like feedback on, click on the "Upload a Document" link to your left on the screen. Browse your computer's file until you find the document you are looking for and click on it. SharePoint's default is to upload the document as a new version; this helps when people start editing it.

7. Click on "OK." This uploads the document. Type in its title and click on the categories and "articles" that it should be related to (see figure 6).

Now you are ready to "check out" a document and make comments on it:

1. Go to the idea that you wish to "check out"—this is the document you just uploaded. Let your mouse hover on the right side of the document's title until a little down arrow shows. Click on it and a drop-down menu appears (see figure 7).

FIGURE 5

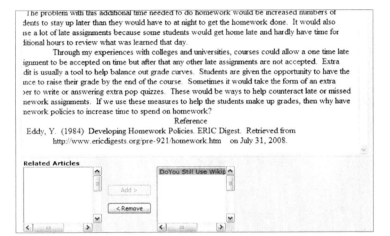

FIGURE 6

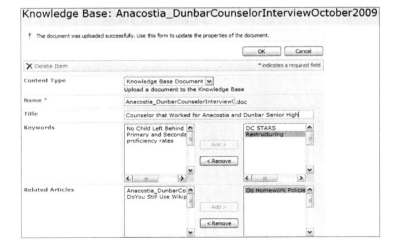

FIGURE 7

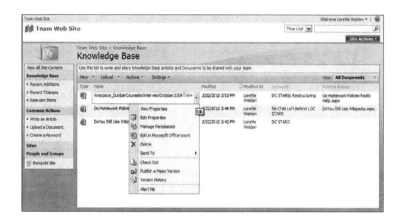

FIGURE 8

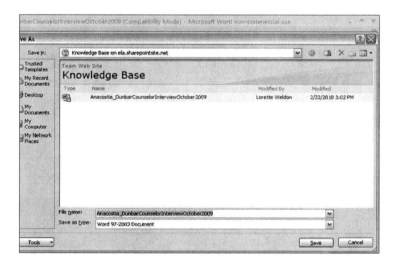

2. Click on "Check-out." To make sure that the document is saved in the space for your library, uncheck the "Use My Local Drafts Folder" option. Now the document is checked out to you. No one else can open the document until you check it back in.

3. Edit the document by clicking on "Edit in Microsoft Office Word" (see figure 7). If you are using SharePoint 2007, Office 2003 will work here. SharePoint 2003 may have some trouble with Office 2007.

4. The document is downloaded on your computer. Make all of the edits you want and then click "Save As." SharePoint automatically connects you to the server that houses the original document. This ensures that you are

FIGURE 9

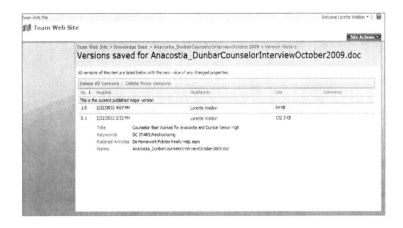

saving the correct document where everyone will be able to find it (see figure 8).

5. You have started a history of changes for the document. Click on "Version History" (see figure 7) to see the different edited "versions" of the document (see figure 9).

6. Check the document back in by closing the document (see figure 7).

Congratulations on making a SharePoint communication portal for staff to share their experiences with each other.

Notes

1. R. DuFour, "What Is a 'Professional Learning Community?'" *Education Leadership* 61, no. 8 (May 2004): 6–11.
2. Lorette S. J. Weldon, "My Virtual Assistant Saves the Day," *Computers in the Libraries* (Information Today), November 2007:18–23.
3. Pew Research Center, *Social Media and Mobile Internet Use among Teens and Young Adults Report*, 2010, www.pewinternet.org.
4. Weldon, ibid.
5. D. R. Sy, *SharePoint for Project Management* (Cambridge: O'Reilly, 2009).
6. D. D. Fowler, "Knowledge Management in Action," *Engineer*, July–December 2008:21–22.
7. D. R. Sy, "5 Reasons Why Executive SharePoint Ignorance Is Not Bliss (Part 1)," November 23, 2009, and "How to Prioritize Business Needs before Implementing SharePoint," December 16, 2009, www.cmswire.com.

28

REAL-LIFE MANAGEMENT USING VIRTUAL TOOLS

Vera Gubnitskaia

LIKE MANY of my colleagues, I often participate in systemwide projects that involve sharing tasks among various departments in the library as well as with people from other businesses and organizations. Like many of my colleagues, I began to realize that doing this using paper management, long meetings, and conference calls was becoming cumbersome and inefficient.

Faced with juggling multiple tasks and the necessity of sharing work with many other players, our library explored different options for utilizing Internet-based sharing resources for everyday tasks and special project management. Let's take several examples of what managers may encounter in their work and demonstrate how we approached these tasks using virtual tools.

EMPLOYEE TRAINING AND DEVELOPMENT

The Orange County (Florida) Library System (OCLS) has a compilation of policies and procedures governing various aspects of library operations. Over time some procedures become obsolete, and others have to be revisited, clarified, and updated. E-mail is sent to employees, revisions are printed and filed, and employee training sessions are conducted. But with the amount of e-mail growing exponentially, our employees are not always able to get their hands on the necessary updates or a procedure quickly. Using a secure log-in to access an internal wiki created with Confluence software, we are able to make documents regarding policies and procedures available from any computer with Internet access. We reduced the volume of e-mail with instructions and reminders, as well as the number of files, folders, and clipboards that organized them. When a procedure is changed or a policy added, the old document is deleted from the site and the new one is uploaded. Staff can sign up for notifications and receive an e-mail every time a specific document is changed.

MANAGEMENT OF LARGE PROJECTS

In 2008, the OCLS was awarded a grant in excess of $100,000 to conduct a new outreach program in the county. The project involved multiple components, including the development of instructional materials and creation of presentations and virtual tutorials. To make instructional materials uniform and to ensure consistency among instructors, a special project wiki was created using PBworks. The site included contact information for all instructors as well as facts about each of the outreach sites including their size, unique characteristics, physical address, and contact information. Team members left comments after each class, describing what was covered during the session. These comments and feedback ensured continuity and smooth flow of the sessions regardless of which instructor was scheduled to present at that center. The wiki also served as a storage facility for PowerPoint presentations, online recorded tutorials, instructional handouts, and other materials that could be utilized by instructors at any time.

GRANT WRITING

Document-sharing tools such as Google Docs are indispensable when you have a team grant-writing project and your team members work miles apart. On several occasions, OCLS staff utilized Google Docs to facilitate team communication and make shared writing more efficient. The project leader divided the application into several parts, such as description of the need, description of the organization, project description, and budget; each team member was assigned a specific part. The collaborators were able work on the same parts in real time and see changes, additions, and updates in the documents as they were made. Considering that in the past we had to e-mail new versions to each team member to ensure that everyone had the most recent update, that real-time collaboration made work easier and prevented mistakes.

SCHEDULING

Google Docs is used by managers to make the scheduling process smoother for employees and managers. The spreadsheet function in Google Docs is utilized to monitor weekly and daily public service and assignment schedules for employees, to coordinate vacation schedules for the division, and to assist managers in coordinating their own schedules.

FUNDRAISING, DONATIONS, AND PRIZE MANAGEMENT

When working on community and programming projects, library staff members often approach local businesses and organizations to ask for donations. To ensure that the same business does not get "hit" too often by our employees, we created a donations spreadsheet using Google Docs. A document owner enters businesses that have been contacted, the date of the contact, and the outcome of the request. Other employees in the system can check with that list before approaching a business or organization.

SUMMER READING PROGRAM

During the summer, the OCLS youth services department coordinates programs, contests, booklists, publicity, and program evaluation for fifteen locations throughout the system. To make it consistent and smooth running, we need to ensure that all locations have access to the same forms, procedures, paperwork, and other documents. Rather than sending hundreds of e-mail to branch representatives and managers, and then asking them share this mail through even more e-mail with the rest of their staff, youth services personnel created pages on the wiki where all summer procedures and documents are stored. Any staff member can access these documents from any computer using a secure log-in. Here are some examples of kinds of documents stored on the wiki:

- contact information for branch staff, especially program liaisons
- list of program presenters and their contact information
- advertising, statistics, and evaluation tools
- booklists and contest forms
- program scripts for story and craft programs

MULTIPART, MULTIPLAYER PROJECT CHECKLIST

It is generally helpful to create a project checklist, something that outlines every detail and every step of the project and notes which of your staff, your colleagues, or your partners are responsible for accomplishing each step. By creating the checklist in Google Docs and providing access to all key players, you allow everyone to see who is responsible for what and when it is due. Your team members then can highlight the parts that are updated, which gives all others an instant view of where the project is at any given moment.

OTHER USES

Our library uses wikis for other purposes. Grant Wiki informs staff about which applications are currently available, if anyone else in the library applied for a grant you are interested in, and the outcomes of previous applications. The Professional Publications wiki posts publishing opportunities. The Professional Conferences wiki offers information on upcoming conferences for the staff who are interested in submitting a proposal. Departmental wikis present information on departments' policies, procedures, and operations.

GRAINS OF SALT

Examine your prospective resource-sharing site and make sure that you are aware of the "small print." For example:

- Is the site that you are planning to use free, or is there a subscription fee? Some give free access for basic services but charge for extra storage. Some give free access to an educational institution but charge a business.
- Is the site secure?
- How many people are allowed to sign as collaborators?

- When using Google Docs, remember that many templates are contributed by users just like you and may have "bugs."
- Google spreadsheet is an excellent tool, but do not expect it to perform like Excel. The same goes for Google Docs document and presentation software. You may be better served by creating the document in a specialty program and then uploading the document to a file-sharing site.
- Free document-sharing sites limit the size of files that you can upload, so they may not be suitable for all of your projects.

Document-sharing and collaborative software offer infinite possibilities for organizations and are especially useful for libraries with limited budgets. As the number and variety of sharing sites grows, so do the opportunities for public libraries to utilize these great tools.

29

SESSION CONTROL SOFTWARE FOR COMMUNITY USERS IN AN ACADEMIC LIBRARY

Jeffrey A. Franks

WITH MORE and more scholarly materials becoming available online and the burgeoning popularity of social networking and gaming, demand for public access computers (PACs) has increased dramatically. At an academic library steadily growing enrollment can add to the demand. In response, some of us have increased the number of available workstations or added circulating laptops. In cases where the only issue is an actual shortage of computers, this is often sufficient. However, for some university or college libraries there may be additional factors. Whether your particular library is large or small, public or private, competition for workstations between students and community users can present a seemingly insurmountable set of issues. Resolving these issues may require creativity and effort, as we saw at the University of Akron (UA).

UA is a medium-sized, state-supported institution in the city of Akron, Ohio. Its urban campus is surrounded by residential neighborhoods, businesses, several social service agencies, and a large homeless shelter. The University Libraries (UL) includes Bierce, the main campus library, and Auburn, the science and technology library. The UL has a long tradition of service to its surrounding community, including borrowing and library use privileges, which complement the collections and services available at the large, state-of-the-art public library located just a few blocks away.

Until recently the UL was able to provide these services without conflict, but two simultaneously occurring factors were to change a long-standing set of harmonious circumstances: the university experienced significant growth in enrollment, and an increasingly large number of community users began to monopolize library PACs. Even with wireless student laptops (150 at Bierce and 60 at Auburn), students often had to wait for an available computer, especially if they preferred to use a hard-wired workstation.

What attracted the large number of community users to the UL? Why did they prefer our PACs over those at the public library? Once we began to analyze these questions, we discovered some surprising facts.

ANALYSIS AND INSIGHT

Our analysis brought several issues to light. A significant number of community users have to use our PACs to access information that is available only through the academic databases we provide; off-campus access is not available to nonaffiliated users. Some community users simply prefer the campus atmosphere. Others are drawn here for the full Internet access; for example, they can view adult-content websites that are unavailable at the nearby public library. And in contrast to the two-hour time computer use limit at the public library, the UL did not limit the amount of time an individual could spend at PACs per day; the growing popularity of social networking and gaming makes unlimited access time highly desirable. Although there are other needs that we meet, these stood out as the main reasons community use had risen so dramatically.

To complicate matters further, some community users presented behavioral problems, requiring the intervention of campus police. The worst offenses included stealing network passwords from students, sharing passwords with others, breaching network log-in scripts, and utilizing a tag-team approach to hold PACs for themselves and their peers. Additionally, some community users displayed loud, disruptive, and at times harassing behaviors. Each of these offenses violates one or more university or library policies.

The situation reached a crucial crossroads during a semester of intense competition for PACs and increased unpleasant encounters with community users. Students registered numerous complaints, staff intervened frequently to quell disputes, and campus police responded to several instances of stolen passwords and network violations. Finally, the student-run newspaper ran an article describing the issue in detail and expressing the opinion that students should not have to compete with community users for PACs.

WHAT TO DO?

Although the UL's management team had discussed possible solutions, the problem escalated in a short span of time, creating a situation that called for swift and decisive action. The dean of libraries created an ad-hoc working group consisting of heads of three departments—library systems, Bierce Library reference, and the Auburn Science and Technology Library—along with the UL's systems administrator, a staff position specializing in technical support. The group's specific assignment was quickly to select and implement an access and session control software solution for the UL. The group was to come up with solutions that would

- develop policy to correspond with the session control solution
- ensure that the new policy did not conflict with existing UA and UL policies
- continue to provide full Internet access to community users
- continue to meet federal depository guidelines
- effectively communicate the new policy to all parties
- ensure common understanding of potential violations
- ensure that UL employees understand proper enforcement procedures

OUR APPROACH

To implement an effective solution, group members would need to work collaboratively with each other and with reference faculty and staff from both libraries. At its first meeting the group divided up the following tasks:

- conduct a broad discussion of the issues with staff from both libraries
- investigate and evaluate access and session control software
- investigate network log-in and authentication parameters and alternatives
- conduct a literature search to determine best practices
- examine existing computer use and community access policies at peer institutions
- designate a limited number of workstations for community users and recommend a time limit
- develop policy and create signage to communicate new guidelines for community users

OUR FINDINGS

Meeting with reference providers from both libraries, the group discovered an acute sensitivity to the needs of community users but also a desire to provide better service to our primary clientele—students, faculty, and staff. Both libraries reached a separate consensus as to the appropriate number of workstations to designate for community use (four at Bierce; no limit at Auburn), and everyone agreed to mirror the public library's two-hour time limit per person per day.

A review of the professional literature on access and session control software and their applications revealed numerous products providing various features, including time management, computer security, reservation systems, and print management. Although most articles discuss public library settings, where these products are widely employed, Richard Wayne's definitive overview of available products and features is applicable to any type of library and is a good starting point.[1] To understand the latest features of any software product, it is best of visit the company website. By visiting company websites and contacting the technical experts for those products that seemed most appropriate, the UL determined that CybraryN (www.cybraryn.com) was the most suitable product for our needs.

The computer use policies of peer institutions, usually available on campus websites, revealed numerous policies similar to those already in place at UA.[2] Reviewing other policies facilitated our understanding of potential violations and reinforced our sense that we were taking appropriate action.

IMPLEMENTATION AND RESULTS

In the end, the UL was able to implement a software solution in just a few weeks. The new policy and procedures were communicated to library staff, and signage posted at workstations clearly defined new time limit parameters. Upon implementation, student response was immediate and overwhelmingly positive, as was the response from library employees. Surprisingly, most community users expressed an understanding of the rationale for the change, and few complaints were received. Some community users, however, were not happy with the new two-hour time limit and have attempted to breach the software. These users are subject to enforcement of appropriate policies and are asked to leave the library. In summary, this solution has resolved a set of issues for the UL, restoring an environment where student needs are met more efficiently.

Notes

1. Richard Wayne, "An Overview of Public Access Computer Software Management Tools for Libraries," *Computers in Libraries* 24, no. 6 (2004): 24–30.
2. Access and Acceptable Use of University Computer and Information Resources Policy: www.uakron.edu/ogc/docs/11–10_11–6-06.pdf. The UL Acceptable Behavior Policy: www.uakron.edu/libraries/bierce_scitech/about/policies/policies_detail .dot?inode=369493.

30

TO FRIEND OR NOT TO FRIEND: THE FACEBOOK QUESTION

Kim Becnel

ONE OF the most interesting results of the recent surge in the use of social media by people of all demographics is its tendency to blur the line between the professional and the personal. As a manager, you have to make a decision about where you stand in regards to this line. Often, the moment of truth comes when an employee sends you a Facebook Friend request. Should you accept? It depends.

THE BIG DECISION

A manager first needs to decide what his or her primary use of Facebook will be. If you want to be able to gripe about work or to communicate information to family and friends that is more personal than what you would feel comfortable sharing with employees (e.g., the scoop on your love life or the details of your latest medical procedure), then you should enact a no-Facebook-Friends-with-coworkers rule and stick to it. Making exceptions only muddies the waters and hurts people's feelings. If you decide to keep your Facebook and work worlds separate, you need a standard reply ready to send when you get the inevitable requests from coworkers. It can be as simple as "Thanks so much for the Friend request. I've decided to reserve Facebook as a personal space to catch up with family and old friends, so I won't be adding any coworkers to my Friends list." You might choose to include your personal e-mail address or ask the declined friend to lunch to be sure he or she understands that your denial is not a personal rejection.

Deciding to keep people you supervise off your Friends list is a completely legitimate stance, and it is one that your coworkers will understand and respect if you apply it equally. However, it is also possible to use Facebook to communicate with old friends and family while building appropriately personal relationships with your staff members. The key is simply to remember who might be listening when you are "speaking." Although this does introduce some limits, you can talk about more than the weather. You can discuss your hobbies, your pets, your pet peeves, your vacation, your favorite books, movies, and restaurants—pretty much anything you consider appropriate for the wide audience you have decided to allow. What you have to leave out: negative remarks about coworkers and your place of work in general and, perhaps, your political leanings (although this is up to you; you may be comfortable making your coworkers aware of your stance on various social issues).

QUICK TIPS

- Do not send Friend requests to people you supervise. You may put them in an awkward position. Wait for them to ask you.
- When you accept a Friend request from an employee, consider adding a note that indicates that you are happy to accept the request, but that, should he or she ever want to de-Friend you for any reason, you will not take it personally.
- If you cannot say something nice (about work), do not post anything at all.
- Always think twice about what you are about to post. Ask yourself—is there anyone in the world, Facebook Friend or not, I would not want to read this statement? If the answer is yes, it is probably best not to post it.
- Do not take it personally if your coworkers elect not to Friend you or even if, at some point, they decide to de-Friend you.
- Whether or not you decide to Friend coworkers, be aware of your privacy settings and set them appropriately for your general account, your status updates, and each set of photos you post.

CHALLENGES

If you do decide to allow folks you supervise into your Facebook universe, there are some definite potential challenges. Be aware of them in advance before you decide to Friend your coworkers and those you supervise, and think about how you would handle them should they arise.

Inappropriate Posts and the Dreaded De-Friending

There will likely be occasions in which a staff member posts a message you wish he or she had not posted. Let's say, for instance, that a certain staff member you supervise writes something negative on your Facebook wall about another staff member you supervise. Perhaps the staff member thinks this is acceptable since the other staff member—the one being criticized—does not have a Facebook account, or at least does not have one that his coworkers know about. In this situation, you would need to write a private message to the complaining staff member, informing her that her post was inappropriate and that you had to delete it. Some staff members would understand, and you could then continue your Facebook friendship; others, however, might have their feelings hurt and remove you from their Friends list. And don't think it doesn't sting to be de-Friended. In any case, you should be prepared to let your staff know if they cross any lines and to endure a de-Friending, or even initiate one, if necessary.

Finding Out Things You'd Really Rather Not Know

Although you may have decided to operate within certain boundaries when you accepted Friend requests from coworkers, be aware that they did not necessarily make the same considered decision. Be prepared to find out things about your staff you may really rather not know. Let's say, for example, you are fairly liberal-leaning when it comes to politics. How will you react when you discover that an employee, or two or three, hold very conservative stances? How will you respond when you teach classes on diversity and cultural sensitivity, and the same staff members who seem to understand you perfectly in class go home and post Facebook statuses that say things like, "For English, press one. If you don't speak English, hang up and call back when you do." Will you be able to evaluate this employee's on-the-job attitude and performance objectively? If not, you may want to reconsider adding employees to your Friends list.

BENEFITS

If you can successfully negotiate the challenges, thoughtful use of Facebook can increase your managerial effectiveness by cultivating positive, and still professional, relationships with employees.

Easy Socialization with Employees

If you are one of those people who finds it impossible to get the members of your department together outside of work, you might find Facebook to be a wonderful tool for some basic socialization. Facebook can facilitate the kind of chatting you might do at the yearly picnic—you know, the one that no one in your department (except you) attends. You can admire pictures of pets and kids, send get-well wishes, commiserate when it is too cold, rainy, hot. Especially if you supervise staff members you do not often see in person, you may find this a most welcome opportunity to show an interest in the lives of your employees and a concern for their welfare. Revealing humanizing (not humiliating) things about yourself further establishes this connection, allowing your employees to show interest in and concern for you.

Publicizing Library Events

If you have a large circle of library Friends, you can send them short promotional posts for upcoming programs. Your Friends can easily hit "share" and repost these items to their own pages to help spread the word.

Now, should you Friend your Mom? I'm afraid that's another discussion entirely.

31

WHY A WIKI? HOW WIKIS HELP GET WORK DONE

Alice B. Ruleman

THE QUINTESSENTIAL wiki is the online encyclopedia Wikipedia—a living document with articles added by anyone and then edited by many. Wikis continually evolve as they generate knowledge. The simple web pages make it easy to access and edit shared documents, and they can be put together quickly and easily. The online process is much less cumbersome than attempting to do joint editing by e-mail. Revisions are tracked, and the group can revert to an earlier version at any time. Multiple pages can be linked together.

HOW TO CHOOSE WIKI SOFTWARE

So many wiki applications are available that it can be difficult to determine which one to select. WikiMatrix (http://wikimatrix.org) is a great tool for comparing features of over one hundred choices. The website directs the user through a series of questions to determine what kind of wiki is needed and then generates a side-by-side comparison. Lombardo, Mower, and McFarland suggest considering these features:[1]

- *cost:* Many wikis are free with a fee-based upgrade for more features.
- *external or internal hosting:* External hosting is web based and easy. This option is more likely to limit the number of users and the amount of storage space. Internal hosting on local servers gives the library more control of the wiki, but technical support is required. Internal hosting provides more flexibility in setup features, security, amount of storage, and number of users.
- *number of participants:* Some free programs limit the number of participants.
- *security restrictions:* Is it a public or private wiki? Do you need to restrict editing privileges? Is editing open on all pages, or are some pages restricted to read only?
- *editing functionality:* Do you want WYSIWYG (what-you-see-is-what-you-get) editing or HTML coding? Does it use a specialized wiki syntax that may be confusing for users without an HTML background?
- *storage:* How much document storage space is needed? A short-term project does not need much; a library-wide wiki with multiple users and groups requires more.

HOW LIBRARIES USE WIKIS

Wikis are flexible Web 2.0 tools that can be used for many purposes by individuals, groups, or organizations. Let's look at some ways real libraries are utilizing them.

Staff and Student Workers: Training and Information

The library at Tarleton State University (Texas) has used a wiki for training student workers since 2007 to provide information about schedules, pay periods, dress code, phone use, safety issues, and departments within the library. The library maintains a separate wiki for staff, which the instruction and outreach department has found particularly helpful.

The technical services wiki at the University of Hartford (Connecticut) houses a training manual for student workers on PBworks. The Colorado Christian College circulation desk chose the same application to post tasks, reminders about policies, coming events, available hours that need to be covered, and notes about the librarian's schedules. Students are required to check the wiki when they arrive and to look for updates throughout their shifts.

Department Wiki

Roanoke County (Virginia) Public Library selected PBworks for several departments in its library system. The technical services wiki houses internal cataloging instructions, processing information, and forms. The young adult and children's wiki proved helpful when branch libraries planned the summer reading program.

Policies and Procedures Manuals

Wikis are well suited for policy and procedure manuals because they are easy to access and revise. The technical services department at Yakima Valley Libraries (Washington) uses SharePoint for cataloging procedures and directions. It no longer needs the binders and notes that previously stored this information. Missouri University of Science and Technology set up a library-wide wiki with sections for each department. Its cataloging department maintains an online manual of local cataloging practices. At the University of Maine, the monograph acquisitions procedures are posted on PBworks. All the staff in the department can access and edit the content. Other departments are restricted to read-only access.

Library Intranet or Resource Page

The University of Central Missouri library uses MediaWiki as a resource page with access to forms, documents, committee and team minutes, and even recipes. The minutes can be opened and edited by team members. Swiki was the tool of choice for Oregon State University, with space for workgroups, committees, and projects.

Internal policies and practices are stored on a wiki at the National Network of Libraries of Medicine. Pathfinders are also included, such as one for free government medical images. The most popular part of the wiki is the travel page, with restaurant and hotel recommendations, since the staff travels frequently.

SOME WIKI APPLICATIONS

- *PBworks*
- *MediaWiki*
- *DokuWiki*
- *TWiki*
- *PmWiki*
- *PhpWiki*
- *Wetpaint*
- *MoinMoin*
- *FlexWiki*
- *XWiki*
- *TikiWiki*
- *WikiWorks*
- *Wikispaces*

Committees and Projects

Wikis are an ideal medium for group members to work together, whether they are in the same building or separated geographically. A SharePoint wiki was used by a committee at Yakima Valley Libraries to brainstorm, create a rough draft, and store minutes.

Event Planning

The Kirkpatrick performance series team at the University of Central Missouri utilizes PBworks to plan student performances in the library. Tasks for each event are listed on the wiki, and color coding indicates if a task is in process or completed.

Workflow Control and Maintenance

The longest-running wiki at the University of Southern Mississippi library functions as a master list of digitized materials that need basic metadata entered. The digitization staff adds titles to the wiki when they are ready for the catalogers. Work in progress and date completed are also recorded.

HOW TO PREVENT WIKI "FADE-AWAY"

Although there are plenty of active, thriving wikis in libraries, sometimes "they just seem to fade away from lack of use," as colleague Nancy Chesik once told me. Successful wikis share at least some of the following characteristics:

- Software is easy to access, navigate, and edit.
- Information is pertinent and has a clear purpose.
- New information is added regularly.
- Training is provided.
- Continued support is given and participation is encouraged.

If you establish a wiki, realize that adoption will take time. Lombardo, Mower, and McFarland suggest that team projects benefit from a designated leader to motivate and keep them on track.[2] A change of habit may be required. A conference wiki has been used with limited success by the Association of Christian Librarians for attendees to ask questions about the location, arrange rides to and from the airport, and give first-timers suggestions. Members are so accustomed to using the active discussion list that they forget to use the wiki.

ADDITIONAL CONCERNS

As useful as wikis can be, there are additional issues that need to be considered.

- External wikis can suddenly disappear from the Internet and may not be a good option for long-term use.
- Although wikis are usually easy to use, staff need to be trained. Do not expect them to jump in on their own.
- Security issues need to be addressed. Who will have editing privileges? How sensitive is the information?
- Formatting is another concern. Wikis do have basic formatting functionally, but they are not as sophisticated as Microsoft Word. Formatting is lost when documents are copied and pasted to or from Word.

Successful wikis fill a real need, but they do require buy-in and participation from the users. This chapter provides some examples of successful wikis in other libraries. How can a wiki benefit yours?

Notes
1. Nancy T. Lombardo, Allyson Mower, and Mary M. McFarland, "Putting Wikis to Work in Libraries," *Medical Reference Services Quarterly* 27, no. 2 (2008): 132–33. doi:10.1080/02763860802114223.
2. Ibid., 137.

PART IV
Staff

32

MILLENNIALS, GEN-X, GEN-Y, AND BOOMERS, OH MY! MANAGING MULTIPLE GENERATIONS IN THE LIBRARY

Colleen S. Harris

CREATING COHESIVE teams and committees that capitalize on the strengths of the age diversity in libraries is both challenging and essential to the long-term success of the library and institution as a whole. Today's libraries have as many as four generations working within them, each with their own unique work styles and worldviews: veterans, baby boomers, Gen-X, and Gen-Y, or Millennials. Knowing the characteristics of each generation brings some insight into the best ways to manage multiple generations in your unit to create dynamic synergies, learning opportunities, and team-building activities and to ensure effective project completion.

TYPECASTING THE GENERATIONS

Individuals inevitably deviate from wide generalizations, but there are characteristic work styles for each generations. Knowing these descriptions, broad as they may be, can help you manage your staff more effectively.

Veterans (b. 1900–1945). As a group, veteran workers generally enjoy structure, abide by the rules, and are most comfortable with conformity and a top-down management style. Largely motivated by verbal or written recognition, awards, and public acknowledgment of success, they are considered the most "loyal" and least likely to switch jobs of the various generations. Veteran workers are also the most likely to prefer to be an expert in their job function rather than a "jack of all trades."

Baby Boomers (b. 1946–1964). Known to work until they drop, the boomer generation outnumbers all other generations. Master networkers, they value relationships over most other work-related values, and instead of vague recognition they prefer status symbols such as titles, raises, and other tangible benefits as rewards for a job well done.

Generation X (b. 1965–1979), Gen-Xers are known to be computer-savvy, skeptical of authority, and strongly preferring work/life balance in their careers. Opportunities to learn and grow are essential for Gen-Xers to be happy in the workplace, and they are likely to leave any work environment that fails to provide those challenges. This generation prefers autonomy in their work to a greater degree than previous generations.

Generation Y/Millennials (b. 1980–1999). The Millennials came of age during a time of technological sophistication and economic turmoil. They exhibit the greatest need to feel that they are contributing to the good of the world with their work. They want personal connections at work and for their managers to value them as individuals in addition to valuing the product of their work.

KNOW YOUR STAFF

Knowing your staff members' preferred working styles not only helps you decide where to deploy them most effectively for productivity but gives you an idea of what skill-building resources you should be offering to keep them engaged and learning. Remember that memo you got from library administration about the recent licensing of self-paced software training? You might want to highlight that opportunity for your staff. Expect to hear interest from your Gen-Xers, who are known to want additional challenges. Do you know which of your staff prefer private acknowledgment of their successes and which would be touched by a thank-you card or official memo? Knowing what motivates your staff helps keep them happy. This means you have to take the time to step out from behind the desk and get to know your staff as people.

FOSTER COLLABORATION

Make sure you are not allowing your staff to segregate by age group, since this reduces the advantages of a lot of synergy. Foster collaboration by consciously building teams to foster collaboration and opportunity for your staff. Your veterans will bring their expertise to the table and be consulted on library functions and processes, boomers can satisfy their need for status by being tapped as team or project leaders, Gen-Xers can broaden their skill sets by serving on several different teams, and Millennials will likely be most interested in the projects and teams they deem most valuable. If you can balance the work that needs to get done with work people truly enjoy, the entire organization benefits.

PEER TRAINING

Don't forget that peer training allows your library to take advantage of staff expertise at any age. An additional benefit of peer-to-peer training is that staff members from different age groups learn how to interact, accommodate, and capitalize on their coworkers' skill sets. Acknowledging the strengths of your staff—which often fall along generational lines—provides you a strategic edge in strategic planning and team building. This means, for instance, that staff have to learn to be sensitive to the technological competency levels of their coworkers if you tap a Millennial to start offering technology training. The best way to foster appreciation of age diversity is through interaction, and with all staff involved in some capacity in training each is able to both demonstrate their skills and learn those of others.

COMMUNICATION IS KEY

Generational differences in communication can have an effect on the entire work environment. Address misunderstandings as they arise and be careful how you communicate both your expectations and new opportunities. Focusing only on high-tech aspects of new work can alienate those less comfortable with technology, and encouraging long work days and weekend work may make younger staff members grumpy. Also, make your staff aware of how they are communicating. Do younger staff make fun of older staff for not being on the bleeding edge of technology? Do older staff frown on the casual dress of younger staff? As a manager, make your expectations of your staff clear, and address attitudes or remarks before they become inflammatory and decrease the productivity and well-being of the workplace.

DON'T MAKE ASSUMPTIONS

Generalizations about groups of people are just that—they cannot take into account the needs and wants of individuals who fall outside the broad brushstrokes of these generational breakdowns. There are baby boomers who are early adopters of every technology you can think of, and some Millennials have yet to discover social networking tools. Some Gen-Xers are workaholics, and some veterans want to multitask and learn various work roles. Don't assume knowledge—or ignorance—of any particular skill on the basis of a person's age.

Managing with an eye toward what motivates members of different generations can give you the tools to advance your library strategically and to assign work in a manner that is both fair and consistent with the desires and goals of your staff. Managing multiple generations while challenging them in terms of their different values and desires offers the rewards of the wisdom of experience and the novel take on traditional functions and processes. The benefits of managing your multigenerational workforce well are many, including reduced staff turnover and a pleasant working environment. How are you capitalizing on the unique blend of ages in your library workforce? How are you making your library a workplace where staff of every age group feel comfortable and valued?

33

HIRING AND TRAINING GRADUATE ASSISTANTS FOR THE ACADEMIC LIBRARY

Erin O'Toole

THE RESEARCH and instructional services department of the University of North Texas Libraries employs eleven graduate assistants (GAs) to provide face-to-face and virtual reference services. Two subject librarians have developed procedures and practices that simultaneously streamline management and motivate the GAs to provide consistently professional reference service. Try these tips for hiring and training to improve your GA program.

HIRING

When you are considering graduate students for employment, their employment histories, education record, and personalities are more important than their fields of study. Students with the following qualifications make the best employees:

- customer service or teaching experience
- passion to help people
- stability in school and employment records
- working knowledge of Microsoft Office and Web 2.0 applications
- outgoing personality

Design your interview with open-ended questions, giving applicants the opportunity to tell you their experiences. Remove jargon from interview questions and add examples of the information you seek, such as these:

- What computer software have you used, such as Microsoft Office, Photoshop, or Dreamweaver?
- Do you have experience with Facebook, Twitter, blogging, or other social networking tools?
- With which electronic library resources are you familiar? Some examples are journal article databases like EBSCOhost databases, encyclopedias, and bibliographic managers.

Many students do not read the job description carefully because they get excited at the prospect of making money. You can eliminate ill-matched applicants and reduce misunderstandings with GAs by explaining the graduate assistantship requirements and department's expectations at the interview. Carefully review a handout of the employment conditions with the applicant. Besides salary, these are the most important facts to cover:

- number of enrollment hours required per semester
- number of work hours required per week and over the year
- requirements for evening and weekend shifts
- activities allowed during shifts
- dress code
- procedures for sick and vacation days
- frequency of paychecks
- details of benefits
- availability of summer and postgraduate employment

NO JARGON

Even if applicants are library and information science students, do not expect them to recognize library jargon in interview questions. When training GAs, be careful to explain any jargon, because they generally will not tell you when they are confused.

Encourage applicants to take the handout home, review it, and contact you with any questions. After completing a set of interviews, wait at least two days before offering a position to allow the applicants time to consider whether the job suits them.

ORIENTATION

Orientation is the time to start motivating GAs to provide excellent reference service by giving them the overall picture of your library system, explaining their vital place in it, and making them feel welcome. Spend about twenty training hours off-desk and include the following activities to promote inclusion:

- Show GAs the locations of restrooms, mailboxes, staff lounge, and lockers.
- Introduce GAs to the department staff.
- Introduce GAs to the administrative assistant who handles timesheet and payroll issues.
- Teach GAs how to use the time clock software.
- Arrange for GAs to visit with an IT employee to learn computer applications and authentication procedures.
- Tour other departments in the library and introduce GAs to staff.
- Give GAs cheat sheets to help them remember the names of library employees.
- Place pictures and welcoming articles about new GAs in your library newsletter.

Spend the remaining time discussing library policies, procedures, and resources. A wiki on the library's intranet is a convenient place to store this information because it can be updated quickly when policies and resources change and accessed easily by anyone in the organization. Create sample patron questions that require GAs to locate the following policies and procedures on the library website:

- services and policies for reference, reserves, circulation, and interlibrary loan
- library hours and calendar
- library building and collection locations
- emergency procedures

New GAs can do resource training independently with tutorials, sample questions, and answer keys that you have stored in a wiki. Be sure to follow up with GAs after the completion of each worksheet and check for comprehension. Academic libraries have more resources than GAs can learn during orientation, so prepare training materials for representative resources:

- FAQs about books and journal articles
- databases with thesauri
- databases from different vendors
- databases with special functions, such as Web of Science
- multidisciplinary reference resources

One of the most difficult resources for GAs to master is the online catalog. Most are not prepared for the intricacies of cataloging. Some features that confuse them are unusual status codes, multiple entries for different formats, and Continuing and Continued By records for periodicals that have changed titles.

ONGOING TRAINING

After orientation, continue training GAs at weekly meetings of one to two hours during the academic year to keep them current on news about university, library, and resource changes. Bring in different presenters from your library and incorporate active learning to keep them interested in the following activities:

- training in multidisciplinary and subject-specific resources
- training in communication and web development software
- training in instructional methods
- practicing resource presentations
- touring library departments
- role playing of reference skills

MAKE A HANDOUT
Whenever you find yourself explaining or recording information for GAs more than twice, make a form or handout. The initial outlay of time and labor is worth the time saved later and the resulting management consistency.

COMMUNICATION

Communication is daily training. GAs need information every day in order to offer outstanding service. Use several modes of communication for different functions: e-mail, wikis, and instant messaging.

Train GAs to check their e-mail on a daily basis, even if they are not scheduled to work. E-mail is the best mode for handling individual issues, such as scheduling conflicts, vacation days, or anything else that requires a personal response. It is also appropriate for sending out deadlines or projects to the entire team.

A wiki is an appropriate tool for pushing information out to GAs and librarians working reference shifts. It is faster for staff to open a wiki page at the shift's start and find reference information there than to sift through individual e-mail for answers. Additionally, all reference staff can add information to these suggested wiki pages:

- reference news—daily events and changes
- class assignments FAQs
- technology and equipment FAQs
- stumpers—unusual reference questions and their answers

Use instant messaging to maintain an open line of communication with GAs who are working reference shifts. GAs can contact librarians about difficult reference questions, desk coverage, problem patrons, and other time-sensitive matters.

You can have a team of enthusiastic, high-performing GAs at your library by following the tips described in this chapter for hiring and training. They will be motivated and loyal because you included them in the library organization, prepared them to do professional reference work, and supported them with multiple modes of communication. The GAs will develop into first-rate future librarians, possibly for your own library.

34

MANAGING FOR EMERGENCIES: WHAT TO DO BEFORE, DURING, AND AFTER DISASTER STRIKES

Sian Brannon and Kimberly Wells

YOUR MOST important tool during an emergency is your staff. A properly trained and prepared staff can provide the experience, knowledge, and energy that is needed desperately during a crisis. It is important to have everyone in your organization prepared ahead of time so they know what is expected of them in an emergency.

COMMUNICATION

All emergency training and preparation is useless if you cannot get important information to your staff. You need a system to get information relayed quickly.

- Gather emergency contact numbers for all members of your staff.
- Prepare a phone tree based on the organizational chart so that supervisors can call their employees and relay relevant information from the top down. It is critical to call everyone, even those employees who are not needed initially so that they understand what is happening and when and where they are expected to report.
- Update this information frequently and keep a copy in your emergency manual.
- Provide employees with emergency contact information for their organization. If you are unable to contact them because the crisis has forced them from their homes or cell phones are out, this gives them someone to call to update their situation.

EMERGENCY MANUAL

A must-have for every branch of your library is a manual detailing procedures to follow. It is recommended that your manual be in a three-ring binder with visible dividers and a table of contents to provide swift and easy access to the appropriate procedures.

One of the first instructions on all procedures should be "remain calm." This reminds the staff to not overreact, to set a good example for those around them, and to let those around them know that there is someone in control of the situation.

Phone numbers in the manual should include home numbers for directors and managers and after-hours numbers for your facilities and technology departments. Additional helpful numbers include Red Cross disaster line, your local mental health/ mental retardation center, and suicide hotlines. Include a staff organizational chart with the emergency phone tree that contains staff contact information. As with all procedures, this should be reviewed regularly to make sure that the numbers are all current, and for staff members it is helpful to have both landline and cell phone numbers listed.

The binder should cover procedures for the following situations:

Medical emergencies. Remind staff not to discuss insurance information with members of the public and not to discuss the cause of any accident or conditions that may have contributed to the cause of an accident. The main concern of the staff should be the well-being of people who have been injured or become ill. The procedure should also state what staff should do after an emergency, such as fill out an incident report form.

Tornados and other severe weather. Remind staff where their "safe areas" are. It is important to let them know under what conditions they should begin moving patrons to this area. All locations should have a weather radio to provide them with the most up-to-date information.

Power outage. Staff should know where flashlights are in their area. Remind them to check the public bathrooms. Only staff trained to handle your electrical system should attempt to trip breakers. Electricity is not something to experiment with.

Flooding. Include basic steps to take regarding electricity and protecting the collection.

Chemical spills and fire. In these cases have staff use cell phones to make the emergency calls so they can quickly leave the building as they are sharing information. Include a chart that shows the location of all fire extinguishers.

Phone/bomb threats. Have a checklist in this section with questions to ask a caller and details to write down regarding their demeanor/voice. Tell staff not to discuss the threat with the public. Also include steps for receiving a written threat or suspicious object on the premises.

Explosions. This is a good place to list some of the signs of a possible gas leak.

Workplace violence

Hostage situations

Evacuation. Identify a safe spot outside of your library that all staff know as a place to meet during an evacuation. Include actual maps of your building in this section if possible. Review this with the staff during regular meetings to make sure all new employees and transfer employees know where to go. Some place that is perfect during the day may have no street lights and thus be unsuitable for meeting in the evening. Have procedures in place about what to do about unaccompanied children.

If your municipality or school has policies associated with any of the above emergencies, copies of those policies should be in your manual as well.

TRAINING

It is important to train staff regularly on what to do in a crisis. The more prepared they are, the more able they are to handle a situation. Panic can set in when nobody knows what is happening, where they need to be, or what they need to do. Training helps keep the situation as calm as possible. There are many opportunities to provide this information:

New employee orientation. Be sure new staff members are aware of the locations of the emergency manual and the emergency supplies. Also be sure to add new staff to the phone tree.

Staff development day. Many locations have one (or more) days during the year on which they train staff on library technologies, updated policies and procedures, and the like. This is a good time to include a program on what to do in an emergency to ensure that everyone is on the same page. Invite a police officer to talk about what to do when a patron becomes violent or the fire department to demonstrate the correct way to use a fire extinguisher. The more questions the staff can ask, the more comfortable they will be in these situations.

Professional meetings. Many state and national library association meetings include programs on disaster preparedness. A member of your staff can attend and bring back ideas to share with managers and coworkers.

Staff meetings. During your weekly (or monthly) staff meetings always make sure to ask if anyone's contact information has changed so that the manual can be updated.

Drills. No matter how well planned ideas are on paper, the best way to tell if something is going to work is to actually do it. This does not work for all situations, but in the case of evacuating the library or taking everyone to the safe room during severe weather a drill can help find holes in your plan. You may discover that the librarians and the circulation staff each think it is the others' responsibility to check the restrooms. This problem can be addressed and fixed before a real crisis occurs.

The nature of an emergency is that things are not going to go as planned. Communication will be difficult and services that you rely on daily may be unavailable.

Training and preparation cannot guarantee that things will go smoothly. But training does ensure that you have done all you can to give your staff the tools they need to save time that could be lost to chaos, materials that could be lost to neglect, and lives.

35

MANAGING LIBRARIANS AND STAFF WITH YOUNG CHILDREN

Holly Flynn

LIBRARIANSHIP IS an aging profession. As older librarians retire, new librarians must replace them. Indeed, the Bureau of Labor Statistics estimates that the profession is expected to grow by 8 percent between 2008 and 2018.[1] It also seems logical that these new librarians will be at an age where they wish to start their own families. Therefore, library administration may soon need to deal with issues of parental leave issues and make their libraries more family-friendly for their employees. As a librarian who has had two children in the past three years, and as the manager of an employee with a young child, I propose several tips for effectively managing personnel from maternity leave through school-age children.

IT BEGINS WITH PREGNANCY

Be prepared to allow for flexible scheduling to work around the realities of "morning sickness," which can happen any time of day. The pregnant librarian may not wish to work at the reference desk first thing in the morning or teach classes at a particular time of day. She may also need to miss some work for monthly doctor's appointments. Before the birth of the baby, you may want to encourage the librarian to work ahead on projects with looming deadlines, create a manual for her particular job duties, and train coworkers to pick up some of her tasks. This way, her responsibilities are covered while she is on leave, and patrons are not inconvenienced.

MATERNITY LEAVE

Familiarize yourself with your institution's leave policies and make sure your employee knows what is expected. The Family and Medical Leave Act (FMLA), federal law that became effective in 1993, gives many employees twelve weeks off for the birth or adoption of a child, but it does not mandate that employers pay any wages during that time. This may vary depending on the person's classification. Faculty-ranked librarians may get full pay for twelve weeks, whereas unionized support staff may not; they may have to rely on vacation accrual. Many new fathers may be eligible for nonmedical-based leave.

RETURNING TO WORK AFTER THE BIRTH OF A BABY

Be flexible about the employee's return date. This could be delayed for medical reasons or childcare issues. Allow the employee to ease back into her job, working half days for a while. The new mother may not want to take on many projects with quick turnaround times right after she returns to work.

Your normally helpful, eager librarian may be sleep deprived and may feel guilty for leaving her new baby at daycare or with a family member. The need for flexibility remains, for the librarian may have to take time off work for well-baby visits to the doctor. Finally, breastfeeding mothers need a private place to pump—it is not recommended that a woman do this in a bathroom. The mother also needs regular breaks to do this, every three hours or so.

AS THE CHILD GROWS

The need for flexibility continues. Children in daycare contract viruses and spread them to the rest of the family, so the parent eventually needs to stay home to deal with sickness. Additionally, home daycare providers may close if they get sick or go on vacation. Make sure you know your institution's policies on staff caring for sick family members, such as whether they must take a vacation day or a family sick day.

It is helpful to let librarians know their schedules well in advance. For instance, try to publish your reference desk schedule monthly. This way, parent-librarians have time to make childcare arrangements for night and weekend shifts, when daycare centers are generally closed. This consideration is of utmost importance to single parents. Advance notice on scheduling is appreciated by everyone on the reference desk, not just those with small children.

You may wish to work out a flexible day for a librarian to work at home, especially if her child's school is closed for a snow day. Many library tasks, from ordering material to updating research guides, can be done remotely. If the person normally staffs a public service point and must be at work, perhaps consider having a "floater" employee who can fill in at a moment's notice.

You may encourage your employee to add you as an emergency contact at her child's school, in case the child becomes ill while the parent is at a workshop or conference. Though you may not be comfortable picking the child up, you may know where the mother is and can contact her on behalf of the school.

Some new mothers may be reluctant to leave their children at home in order to attend national conferences. Give the librarian the option of going for only a day or two, or if possible offer a stipend for her to take her family with her. Value the librarian's contributions to local or statewide organizations as you would with a larger association and provide opportunities for online professional networking. Many national associations now offer a virtual component to their annual conferences.

Additionally, set guidelines about bringing children to work and enforce them. They may vary depending on the type of library. For instance, children of employees at a public library may be able to sit in the children's section for a short time, whereas there may be no age-appropriate place at other types of libraries.

Finally, you may want to discuss other flex-time issues. During my second pregnancy, I worked with management to secure an academic year appointment in which I worked only a total of nine months per year. Other academic librarians still working their way through the tenure system may wish to investigate stopping the tenure clock, if possible. Make sure the employee knows all of the implications, from keeping health care benefits to reorganizing her job to get everything done in a shorter period of time.

Allowing for flexibility in the library workplace has many positive benefits, and not just for new parents. A fair flex-time policy, including publishing schedules well in advance, is appreciated by everyone. People who work in flexible environments are often happier, more loyal workers. Once a librarian has a child, her priorities may change a bit. Whatever the circumstance, having a supportive supervisor and a flexible, family-friendly workplace helps ensure high productivity.

Note

1. Bureau of Labor Statistics, U.S. Department of Labor, *Occupational Outlook Handbook*, 2010–11 edition, "Librarians," www.bls.gov/oco/ocos068.htm.

36
MENTORING GRADUATE ASSISTANTS IN THE ACADEMIC LIBRARY

Erin O'Toole

THE RESEARCH and instructional services department of the University of North Texas Libraries is committed to mentoring the library and information sciences graduate students who staff our face-to-face and virtual reference services. Two subject librarians have developed a formal mentoring program to grow the graduate assistants (GAs) from library newbies to entry-level librarians in the course of a year. The mentoring activities occur in the context of weekly meetings with the GA team.

The GAs have been successful in securing jobs within six months of graduation, even in a depressed economy. The library also reaps benefits because the appreciative GAs are dedicated employees, and in their new jobs they promote the reputation of the libraries and extend our network. The activities described in this chapter effectively prepare graduate students for professional librarianship.

PERFORMANCE DOCUMENTATION

When GAs join your organization, give them binders in which they can gather training materials and project documentation. Explain to them that professional academic librarians prepare something similar for annual evaluations and that the documentation helps them prepare for interviews. You can give them some extra guidance by putting labeled dividers into the binder for performance plan, evaluations, documentation, and training.

PERFORMANCE PLANNING

Start mentoring GAs immediately after orientation to your department by having them create a performance plan. Explain that this activity prepares them for drafting annual performance agreements. The plan also helps you assign tasks consistent with the GAs' career aspirations.

Give GAs a week to craft two to three goals each for career and work, with one or two objectives for each goal. Then edit the documents and meet with GAs individually to discuss the performance plans. Be ready to suggest professional development activities to support their goals. GAs may not be aware of the following options, which are usually accessible and affordable for students:

- training in technology, instruction at work
- doing library projects in their areas of interests
- interviewing librarians that share their career or research interests
- taking human-resource courses on campus
- joining discussions lists
- joining subject area or library professional organizations
- publishing reviews or presenting posters
- attending workshops or conferences

After the meetings, have GAs revise their performance plans and return them to you for a final review. The GAs should place the finalized plans in their binders, and you should put copies in your personnel files to consult over the year. To encourage GAs to follow through with their objectives, consider making their progress a factor in their evaluations.

INTRODUCTION TO CAREERS

PROVIDE SAMPLES

Younger graduate students have had little or no experience preparing a performance agreement, documenting their work, or applying for a professional job. Therefore, they need substantial guidance in the form of sample documents to facilitate understanding.

Take advantage of departments and librarians at your institution to introduce GAs to careers within librarianship. Tours of library departments at which employees explain their work and roles in the library overall are enlightening for budding librarians. Ask individual librarians to visit GA meetings and describe their average work day, how they prepared for their careers, and what opportunities exist for employment and advancement.

To recruit speakers from outside academic librarianship, use your contacts in the community and professional organizations. Most are happy to share their experiences with GAs. If distance is a problem, consider having the speaker meet with the GAs through chat or classroom software such as Wimba.

JOB HUNT PREPARATION

As GAs approach graduation, increase the number of activities that prepare them for job hunting. First, introduce them to the multitude of professional development resources available, which you can also use to prepare lessons:

- librarians in your organization
- professional development books at your library
- career counseling on campus
- professional development websites, e.g., LibGig.com
- professional development workshops, or services at conferences

- job listings, e.g., ALA JobLIST, state library associations' job listings
- library discussion lists that post jobs

The next step is practicing the components of looking, applying, and interviewing for librarian positions. Lead these activities in the order below to mimic the job-hunting process:

1. Finding job descriptions suited to the GAs' level of experience

2. Writing cover letters in response to job descriptions

3. Writing resumes or CVs

4. Learning to teach a class about library resources

5. Preparing handouts for classes

6. Answering interview questions

7. Drafting thank-you letters to interviewers

Review the students' products and give them feedback on their efforts. This need not be done individually; there are usually common mistakes that can be addressed with the entire group.

PREPARATION FOR THE REAL THING

Mentoring continues as GAs eventually apply for jobs. Make yourself available to proofread cover letters and resumes before they are sent off. When GAs advance to the phone interview stage, make sure to remind them to not use a cell phone because reception may be poor or inconsistent, and to make sure there will be no noise or distractions during the interview, such as pets, children, or nearby construction.

ONLINE RESOURCES

Wondering when you will have the time to locate professional development resources for GAs? Look no further than the portal "100+ Job Resources for Librarians" at www.collegeathome.com/ blog/2008/06/04/100-job-resources -for-librarians/.

Finally, when GAs are invited for on-site interviews, you and the other GAs can assist with preparation. For GAs who might need it, offer advice on how to dress appropriately for interviews. Conduct mock interviews if they desire them. Arrange locations and times when GAs can practice the presentations they will do at on-site interviews. Open the presentations to GAs and other library staff so that students can practice in front of an audience and answer impromptu questions; afterward, you can critique the presentations and make suggestions. Pick only the areas of the presentations that need the most work; you do not want to overwhelm GAs shortly before their interviews.

Inevitably, some GAs are not invited for interviews or offered jobs. Create an environment of support for GAs from the start of mentoring by making it clear that job hunting is not easy and that one is more likely to fail than succeed on the first few tries. Use the setbacks as opportunities to further advise GAs on improving their presentation and interviewing skills.

TOO MUCH TIME?

Are you thinking that mentoring sounds too time-consuming as you read this chapter? Mentoring is a big commitment, but your coworkers can help with planning and leading different activities. You can also take on just a few activities; some mentoring is still better than none. And think about this: Do you want to be proud of your profession ten years from now? Then someone has to pass wisdom on to up-and-coming librarians.

AFTER THEY GRADUATE

Once GAs graduate and leave your library, you still have a mentoring role to play. If they have not secured jobs yet, you can alert them to job postings and proofread cover letters and resumes. For those who have jobs, you can let them know that you are available to give advice. It is reassuring for them to have an ally outside work to answer their "stupid" questions.

Why continue mentoring librarians who are no longer in your employ? Over the course of their assistantships, they have become your colleagues. You will care how they progress in their careers and be proud of their contributions to the profession. And one day they will start sharing contacts, resources, and knowledge with you. With each GA you send off, your library's network broadens and its access to resources increases. There are no losers with mentoring.

37

NEW EMPLOYEE ORIENTATION

Bradley Tolppanen and Janice Derr

A STRONG orientation program for new staff members at the start of their employment is a key ingredient for their success. At the outset of the new person's employment, the library manager can set the tone and get them off to a good start. Although orientating a new employee can be a time-consuming exercise, it is time well spent.

PREPARING FOR A NEW EMPLOYEE

In the days before a new employee starts at the library, the manager should prepare for her arrival and plan out her first day and week of employment. Among the preparations that should be undertaken, the new staff member's work area should be prepared. The area should be filled with the necessary office supplies. The employee's computer log-ins, e-mail account, and telephone should be set up so that she can start working right away. All of this goes a long way toward making the new person feel like a member of the organization.

The library manager should remember to confirm that the new employee knows when and where she will arrive on her first day. If the manager cannot be there to meet her, a staff member should be designated to do so. The current staff should also be told in advance about the new hire coming aboard and what duties she will be performing. This ensures that everyone is expecting the person and can make her feel welcome when she arrives.

THE FIRST DAY

A new hire is often nervous on his first day of work and can quickly feel overwhelmed. The orientation program prepared for him should help him feel comfortable. A detailed schedule of the first day and general schedule of the first week allows him to know what to expect. The manager should try to avoid cramming too much into the first day. Also, the first day should not be too boring for the new staff member. Having to read a thick procedures manual all shift makes the day seem like an eternity.

After meeting and welcoming the new employee on his first day of work, the library manager should provide a copy of the schedule of the day and explain what he will be doing. A set of handouts can also be provided, consisting of maps of the building, fact sheet for the library, organizational chart of the staff, and other library brochures.

The first day of the orientation program should include the following:

introductions of supervisors and staff

building tour (including restrooms and break room)

separate meetings with all supervisors

explanation of basic details, such as work schedule, breaks, pay details

reading the safety procedures

time for the new employee to settle into the assigned office space

manager meeting with new hire at the end of the shift

On the first day, the new person should be given a genuine library task so he feels he is actually contributing; this also provides a break from the orientation. The task assigned can be a simple one that does not require much training before plunging in, such as opening the incoming mail.

SETTING THE TONE WITH A NEW EMPLOYEE

On the new staff member's first day, the manager should take the time to meet with her individually. In this meeting the manager should set the tone for the employment. In a relaxed manner, the manager should explain the mission of the library as well as the specific duties of the position.

Some future problems can be avoided if the manager clearly explains on the first day what is expected of the new employee. Tell her what she must do to succeed in the position. Do not make any assumptions in this regard. It is better to tell her on the first day that she must arrive on time prepared to start work than have to have a conversation later about being late.

As a supervisor you should be as specific as you can with your new employee about how you expect her to perform on the job. If you want to make changes within your department, now is your chance; you have a new person in front of you who is willing and able to do the job the way you want it done. Keep in mind that you are not just expressing your expectations, you are providing this person with directions on how to be successful in her position.

It is important to not let this conversation get too one-sided. Be sure to give your new employee ample time to ask questions. It is also helpful to establish an open-door policy with new staff members so that they feel comfortable coming to you for both small questions and larger issues. Establishing the expectations of the position and creating a good line of communication are crucial to the relationship with new employees. The manager should follow up with a new hire frequently during the first week and the weeks that follow.

TRAINING NEW STAFF

The training of the new person can fully begin on the second day of his employment. If the library manager is not to provide the training, a staff member or staff members should be designated to take the lead. A checklist of tasks to learn is helpful in the training. Let the new hire know that, although you are bombarding him with information, you do not expect him to remember it all; it will be repeated again at a later date. Give your new employee a time frame, usually a couple of weeks, to master these new tasks, and schedule a time to meet back with him. If he does not feel confident that he can do every task on the list by the time of that meeting, then you both know where there has been a gap in the training and it can be remedied.

A manager should not assume too much knowledge on the part of the new staff member. Even with a person who comes with library experience, the manager should start with the basics. This is especially true in entry-level positions. With a new entry-level person in circulation, for example, find out if he comprehends the call number system. If he does not, he can be trained on it. The training should start with the basics and build from there. During the training period, the new hire should not be expected to spend all shift learning new information. As on the first day, he should be allotted specific tasks so that he can feel like he is getting something useful done. As the new person learns more he can make a transition, either quick or gradual, from spending most of his day training to spending most of his day getting work done.

Orienting and training a new employee takes time and patience, but a good orientation makes for a good employee. The more time you invest in newcomers in the beginning, the quicker they are able to become productive parts of the library.

38

DISCRIMINATION IN EMPLOYMENT: AN OVERVIEW FOR LIBRARY MANAGERS

Michael A. Germano

LABOR AND employment litigation is by far the most common type of lawsuit that businesses, government agencies, and nonprofit organizations are required to defend against. Disputes in the context of employment can result in significant costs, and not just the direct ones related to fines, settlements, or verdicts. Litigation itself is an expensive undertaking. Lawsuits involving labor and employment claims can also produce indirect costs related to lost productivity and work hours as employees are deposed, required to attend hearings, or take the time to produce discoverable documents. Additionally, there is the very real and negative impact to workplace and employee morale caused by claims or even the perception of worker mistreatment. Employment litigation creates a battlefield as employers and employees are drawn into what usually amounts to a protracted dispute that typically has no clear winner.

Finally, there is the significant cost to an organization's reputation when liability for mistreatment of employees is found.

From job posting to interviewing to hiring and termination, there are multiple opportunities for a claim of discrimination to arise. For many managers, especially newly minted ones, the concept of discrimination in employment usually remains on the periphery of job function until something goes drastically wrong.

PERSONAL LIABILITY FOR MANAGERS

It is bad enough for a manager to engage in actions that can create liability for an employer, but employment discrimination can also result in personal liability. A manager can be sued as an individual and, if found liable, can lose home, bank account, investments, and personal property. Additionally, the employer may not have a duty to defend—meaning the manager could be on the hook for legal costs as well.

Employment discrimination represents one of the largest exceptions to the common law rule of at-will employment. The theory behind employment-at-will is based on a leveling of the playing field between employer and employee. Succinctly, employment-at-will recognizes that, though employees can change jobs at any time, employers may require the same level of flexibility in terms of managing workers. Employment-at-will does, however, have significant limitations, mostly in the form of an employer's right to terminate employment. Specifically, at-will employment can be terminated for any reason as long as that termination does not violate an employment contract; a public policy exception; or a federal, state, or local law. Employment discrimination falls under the third category since there are a variety of laws from federal, state, and local jurisdictions that protect a large number of people with specific characteristics from discrimination in an employment context. Here are the most common areas or characteristics protected by federal and state laws:

- gender
- ethnicity
- national origin
- pregnancy
- disability
- age (over 40)
- religion
- citizenship status
- bankruptcy or bad debts
- military service including anticipated deployment
- genetic conditions

In addition, many state and local governments have extended protections to gay, lesbian, and transgender employees and applicants as well as those with medical conditions that may not fall under state or federal laws that define disabilities. The important lesson here is that protection from discrimination in employment can be covered by any jurisdiction in which the employee works including the city, county, state as well as country via federal laws. Additionally, employment discrimination can apply to virtually any incident where one employee is treated differently from another if it appears that different or disparate treatment is due to the employee's characteristic or status as a member of one of the protected groups.

Unfortunately, fear of litigation has resulted in a significant number of managers assuming there that is an affirmative requirement to hire or retain a person who falls within one of the protected classes of employment, despite that person not being the best qualified or not performing adequately. Nothing could be further from reality. Provided managers act prudently and document their actions at every stage in order to demonstrate their compliance with current discrimination law and the protections offered, an applicant can legally be denied employment or an employee terminated despite being a member of a protected group.

For example, a library manager could deny employment to someone with a disability if the main function of the job required lifting or pushing a heavy book cart. If there is a job-related need that is tied to a main function of the prospective employee's work, and a disability prevents meeting that need and reasonable accommodation is not realistic, then there is a business necessity limitation on a claim of employment discrimination in hiring. The business necessity exception is narrow, but it does offer a defense against discrimination if there is a reasonable business justification for either intentional or unintentional discrimination. As far as termination for performance goes, there is no discrimination if the termination is based on neutral performance management standards that have nothing to do with the employee's membership in a protected class. As long as poor or inadequate performance is managed in a fair, legal, and neutral way as well as consistently and clearly documented, a claim of discrimination can be avoided.

As a frontline manager, or one with direct supervisory responsibility, acquainting yourself with applicable labor and employment law before problems erupt is critical. Library managers are no exceptions to this rule. Managers in libraries supervise a wide variety of employees including professionals, paraprofessionals, and staff. Workers can be hourly or salaried, full- or part-time. The diversity of job functions, descriptions, and work requirements all make the likelihood of dispute very real for a manager in a supervisory role over other library employees.

Given the current economic climate with layoffs, furloughs, and reductions in hours becoming all too commonplace, the chances for disputes arising out of perceived or real discrimination are rising. When any job action takes place that affects individuals or groups, it is useful for managers to step back and examine the process from all potential sides. Taking a few moments to examine the impact of making or denying an offer of employment to a candidate, a change in job duties, a restriction in employee benefits or, especially, a termination or layoff is critical to managers

KNOW THE LAW

Some great resources are available to help you educate yourself as a manager in order to avoid problems before they arise:

- Gibson, Paul C., and Kathryn Piscitelli. 2009. *CCH Basic Employment Law Manual for Managers and Supervisors.* 4th ed. Chicago: Wolters Kluwer Law and Business/CCH.
- Guerin, Lisa, Amy DelPo, and Lisa Guerin. 2009. *The Manager's Legal Handbook.* 5th ed. Berkeley, Nolo.
- FindLaw: http://employment.findlaw.com
- U.S. Department of Labor: www.dol.gov
- U.S. Equal Employment Opportunity Commission: www.eeoc.gov
- Workplace Fairness: www.workplacefairness.org

who wish to stay on the right side of the law, especially as it relates to employment discrimination. A good rule of thumb, besides the defense of an offense in the form of vigorous self-education, is to practice common sense and think about any negative perception surrounding choices or decisions, especially those that have a negative impact like firing or reducing hours. And along with that commonsense approach, document, document, and then document again.

39

OBTAINING COMPLIANCE FROM UNDERPERFORMING EMPLOYEES: TALKING IT THROUGH

Terry Ann Lawler

ONE OF the many roles of the manager is to maintain and promote a safe, productive work environment. That manager in Library X with the smoothly running department, happy, efficient employees, and hassle-free workdays probably did not start out that way. Transforming a team into a well-oiled machine takes some elbow grease. Although talking to your employees about their performance issues is difficult, it is a challenge that enables you to learn and grow. Expanding your comfort zone makes you a better, more successful manager.

After you have made it clear to your staff what sort of behavior you expect and what the policies are, you may still have employees who are not complying. Perhaps you have an employee who does only half the work the other employees are doing. Other examples include tardiness (excepting those under family medical leave), constant bickering, inaccuracy, and refusal to cooperate. Whatever the issue, you know you need to meet to deal with these problems.

BEFORE THE MEETING

The first step to tough employee talks is preparedness. Take a deep breath. Call a mentor. Call your human resources department. Make notes on advice given and use them to plan ahead. Have your library's policies on hand and be familiar with them. Practice, practice, practice. Engage in role play and rehearse phrasing policies in your own words. Make a list of possible openings to the conversation with your employee. For example, "It has been brought to my attention that _____. Please tell me about it." Practice responding to the employee in different ways.

The second step is to plunge in. Putting off or ignoring complaints from staff and customers and hoping they will go away give the impression that these concerns are not real or not worth discussing. Even though you are just worried about how to handle the issue, you may be perceived as insensitive or even inept. Acting quickly on an issue builds trust and sets boundaries. Pick a time to meet with your employee and stick with it. You may want to meet first thing in the morning, or right before closing. Your employees deserve to know

THINGS TO REMEMBER

It is not a sign of weakness to ask for help.

immediately that their performance is lagging. This gives them the opportunity to correct the issue and grow.

DURING THE MEETING

State your purpose clearly. Be sure to avoid blaming. You are assessing the employee's actions and work results. You are not assessing the employee's personality. Be careful not to display an accusatory attitude. Instead, focus on facts and your concern for the employee's individual success and the teams' success. Keep it short. Assess only one matter at a time. State the problem clearly, briefly, and fairly. Give all important facts: date, place, persons involved, and so on. Explain why it is important. You should have all necessary information in note form in front of you. Some helpful starters:

- "It has come to my attention that . . ."
- "I am hoping for your help in resolving a problem . . ."
- "I was a bit disconcerted to hear that . . ."

What not to say? Avoid using sarcasm or accusations. Never abuse, recriminate, or blame. Remain unemotional and try not to repeat yourself.

What if it is a really sensitive issue? Although it is important to be nice, do *not* give in to the temptation to sugarcoat, come up with code words, or otherwise dilute the situation. Be very specific—but also remember to be kind. Soften your tone of voice. For example: "Jennifer, this is a sensitive issue and very difficult for me to bring up, but it has come to my attention that there have been complaints about your body odor." You can demonstrate care and compassion while sticking to the facts. Once you have broached the subject, you can begin to focus on resolving the issue. Offer your assistance in any way that is appropriate.

Next, just listen. After you have stated the purpose of the meeting and given the details as they were reported to you, it is time to let the employee speak. Give him an opportunity to explain. Do not interrupt. Take notes if you need to. Ask questions for clarification only.

Your employee may surprise you and not react in the manner you expect. A stoic and quiet employee may get upset and yell or cry. Regardless of the employee's reaction, stay on track. If you feel that the employee is getting off track, use a guiding phrase or question to get her back to the issue at hand. You can offer a short break so that she can compose herself if necessary. Remind the employee that you are not assigning blame, you are there to help. Remember, your goal is to coach. To get new behavior, you must identify ways to stop the old behavior.

Come to an agreement. After your employee has said everything he wants to say, formulate a plan regarding improvement. Suggest a strategy for the employee to improve. Perhaps you can offer some role playing. Sign the employee up for a class or job shadow. Ask your employee what he thinks he can do to improve the situation.

Explain that now that you have talked, future incidents of the same nature will result in disciplinary action. Make sure to document every meeting with every employee as well as any agreements you have come to.

Some helpful phrases:

- "I know you will want to see that such an incident does not occur again."
- "I am confident that we can resolve this matter to our mutual satisfaction."
- "Let me know what you are doing to improve things."

AFTER THE MEETING

Follow up. Set a time for your employee to meet with you again in a few weeks or a month. Require that your employee provide you with a report about the agreed upon strategy. Is it working? How? What changes has the employee implemented? What were the results? What can she do differently now? Providing timely and meaningful feedback is a must. Employees are more likely to stay committed to results when they know how they are doing.

THINGS TO REMEMBER

No one was ever sorry that they overdocumented a situation.

Reward progress. When you see success, remember to keep the momentum going, reward small improvements, encourage more growth. Publicly acknowledge your employee for their nonprivate successes by using a "kudos" board or mentioning progress at a regular meeting. Show that you have sincere and genuine interest in all of your employees by staying involved in their development.

Speaking to your employees about their performance is an essential supervisory duty. It need not be as difficult as you think. Being prepared, acting quickly, and implementing policy all help. Remember to listen and offer constructive solutions. Follow through to see if they worked. And do not forget to document, document, document. Using these methods improves your employees' performance and creates a more relaxed environment for all staff—not to mention making your job easier in the long run.

40

PLANNING FOR CHANGE: ENSURING STAFF COMMITMENT

Jason Kuhl

ANYONE WORKING in libraries knows that this is a time of great change in our profession. Information technology has opened new doors; innovative libraries are redefining the role they play in their communities. Sooner or later, every manager finds himself or herself in a situation that requires change; how well staff support the change goes a long way toward determining its success.

Four components critical for ensuring staff commitment are laying the proper groundwork, involving staff in planning and implementation, communicating effectively, and analyzing results and making the necessary adjustments. Our experiences at Arlington Heights (Illinois) Memorial Library can flesh out these strategies.

LAYING THE GROUNDWORK FOR CHANGE

The first step in implementing any change is to build a solid foundation for it. Staff are unlikely to buy in to a change they think is unnecessary or does not support the library's philosophies and values. To lay an effective groundwork you must define your organizational goals and values, analyze existing processes and services in light of those values, and present results to highlight needs.

Start broad when defining your organizational values. Your library should have a set of core principles; these may be written and formally defined or a more informal part of your organization's culture. Everyone should know them and understand how your services relate to them. If you are a manager of a smaller unit within a library, you may not have been involved in defining the overall philosophy, but you should define a vision for your department to fit in with it.

Spend some time discussing these values with your staff. Understand that the best reinforcement is to make sure your own actions are guided by your organization's philosophies. Success depends on everyone understanding how their work relates to the library's goals; do not shortchange this step.

One of the focuses at the Arlington Heights Library in 2009 was defining the future of our reference department. To begin laying out our foundation, we created a humorous presentation called "Get R.E.A.L.! A Vision for the Arlington Heights Memorial Library's Reference Collection," which outlined a model for a "Relevant, Efficient, Accessible, and Lean" collection. It was presented and discussed twice, once to the reference librarians and once to the library's management team.

Look at how your procedures and processes contribute to your vision and goals. Sometimes it is easy to see where change is needed; other times you need to look over a longer period. Be sure to gather data and present it to staff and key personnel. Remember, you are laying groundwork at this stage, not proposing solutions. At Arlington Heights, we knew that the two most significant areas of the reference department were its service model and its collections. We collected data to analyze those areas:

- annual reference statistics dating back ten years
- twelve months of reference question statistics broken down by type of contact (telephone or in-person), day of the week, and hour of the day
- internal-use statistics for reference books dating back several years
- statistics of reference book use by librarians

INVOLVING YOUR STAFF

Staff should play a role in every aspect of your project, from generating the idea to planning and implementation. Change comes most easily to those who have a role in orchestrating it. Challenge staff to help define your unit's needs in light of your organization's vision, then let them help you find ways to meet those needs. Think of different ways to give staff ownership of the change; perhaps a staff workgroup can be in charge of one aspect of a project.

Staff was involved in all aspects of the Arlington Heights project:

- Data was discussed at department meetings.
- A workgroup focused on the details of constructing and staffing a department call center.
- We used online surveys to seek input about specific items in the collection.

COMMUNICATING EFFECTIVELY

Communication is critical to ensuring a smooth change. It needs to be frequent, consistent in message, and mutual. Consider multiple methods of communicating, including individual discussions with staff members, group discussions with all staff, written communication, and technological solutions.

Issue regular updates and encourage staff to ask questions. Consider setting up a project blog—a great way to issue updates, seek input, and encourage discussion. Make the process as transparent as possible; staff are less likely to back a project if they feel information is being withheld. Consistently reinforce how the project fits in with the library's stated vision. Share the implementation time line in advance; staff can point out potential problems you may have overlooked. If the project could generate questions from the public, provide a list of basic talking points and give staff clear direction on how to handle additional inquiries. And do not hide problems; staff appreciate candor and can help find solutions.

In the Arlington Heights project, we focused on several methods of communication:

- A weekly e-mail kept members of the department updated and provided a way to solicit feedback.
- Supervisors in the department spoke one-on-one with their direct reports.
- A portion of every department meeting was dedicated to questions about the project.
- Updates were issued on a library-wide blog.

EVALUATION AND ADJUSTMENT

Good management of change does not end when a project is implemented. You should always build in a means to determine the success of your change. This may include statistics, patron or staff comments, or observations. Continue communicating; share the positive results and the negative ones. There will be problems you did not anticipate; seek staff input and make the appropriate changes. If staff know the project is an evolving process instead of a fait accompli, they are more likely to support and commit to improving it.

The Arlington Heights project resulted in substantial changes to our staffing model and to the breadth and organization of our collection. Results have been overwhelmingly positive; usage statistics have increased an average of 27 percent since implementation. Staff receive monthly updates highlighting these positive results. We keep a log of problems at all service points and discuss issues recorded on the logs at monthly department meetings. Several adjustments have come out of these discussions and further improved service.

KEYS TO REMEMBER

Change is not easy; keep these points in mind:

- Define organizational goals and values; they are the foundation for change.
- Be consistent in your message; all decisions should stem from your stated vision.
- Spend time collecting data to establish your needs; not all are easily identified.
- Have evidence to back up your findings; you need to be able to demonstrate the need for change.
- Include all levels of staff every step of the way; staff most readily accept a change they help orchestrate.
- Communicate often; keep staff in the loop.
- Encourage discussion; staff need to know that their concerns are being heard.
- Be transparent; do not hide the process or negative results.

- Know how to assess your project; you need to be able to define a successful result.
- Fix the problems; no plan is perfect.
- Continue to communicate and seek input; the project does not end at implementation.

As a manager, you will one day be required to oversee change in your library. Getting staff to buy in will go a long way toward determining the success of the project. Change is rarely easy, but adhering to basic principles as you manage change will help ensure that staff support your change and leave your library better prepared for the challenges that lie ahead.

41

SHADOW AND LEARN: KNOWING YOUR STAFF

Robin Shader

SHADOWING IS working side-by-side with a staff member while that person performs his or her normal duties. It is a great way to learn exactly what a day in the life is like for individual staff members. Shadowing has many benefits: You get to know your staff, their talents and frustrations. It facilitates communication between frontline staff and management. Management gains a better understanding of the day-to-day issues of staff. Key information needed for decision-making processes is more available. Areas where staff training is needed become apparent.

GETTING STARTED

Creating a shadowing program is a three-step process; preparation, selection, and education. First, decide how much time you can realistically spend with staff. Scheduling an eight-hour session might be difficult and, with part-timers, could require more than a day. Half a day, about four hours, seems to be enough time to get a sense of the workload. Whatever you are able to do, try to make the length of time consistent so staff do not feel they are being treated differently. If a part-timer works only nights and weekends, make time to shadow that person on a night or weekend. Do not ask staff to change their schedule to fit yours.

To prepare for selection, simply get a list of all staff members, separate each name, and put the names in an envelope. Ask someone to pull out one name, then speak to that person and his or her supervisor to schedule a session. It is important to have someone else pull the name so that staff feel certain the selection is random. If an upper-level manager suddenly announces that she is going to shadow Ms. Smith, Ms. Smith may feel she has done something wrong. Developing and communicating a random selection process, especially at the start of the program, are essential. Avoid any selection process that appears sneaky or makes it seem that you have created this program for the purpose of spying on staff.

SHARE WHAT YOU LEARN

There will be some who are suspicious of your motives, so educate staff about your reasons for shadowing. Communicate what you have learned during the experience and what you are doing with this information. To facilitate this, I created our Shadow and Learn blog. All staff members are encouraged to read and comment on the postings. Use the communications tool that works best for you.

Another good reason to share your experience is that staff throughout the system learn what their coworkers in other departments do. Do most staff members know what the switchboard operator does each day? Do public service staff know what is involved in filling an interlibrary loan request? Do your staff members sometimes express the belief that their department works harder than others? Use shadowing to set the record straight.

KEEP SHADOW SELECTION RANDOM

Use a selection method that lets the staff know this is random and you are not targeting specific people. You might ask the current shadowee to select the name of the next shadowee. Always have another staff member draw the name of your next shadowee.

Shadowing has been especially helpful to me as a new administrator, as a reminder to never assume we have consistent procedures across the system and to learn on which procedures staff need training. Observing a staff member providing incorrect information about the library card registration process, for example, provides an opportunity to teach the correct way and to note that this might be an area where refresher training should be provided. This is not an opportunity to criticize staff for doing something wrong but an opportunity to address problems, both big and small, that create barriers to service. It is an excellent way to build trust and share knowledge. Something is learned during every shadowing session.

GETTING TO KNOW YOUR STAFF

A shadowing program helps you get to know your staff on a deeper level. You can learn about their talents and strengths related to their job and what motivates them. In a medium-to-large library, the amount of time an administrator spends with frontline staff is probably little to none. Shadowing is a structured program that creates opportunities to work with staff you might otherwise never work with.

BENEFITS TO MANAGEMENT

When management sees the need to make a change, staff members who perform the work should be involved in the planning process. When a frontline staff member makes a recommendation for change, management needs to know if the suggestion is the best course of action. Shadowing is one method of facilitating this communication. Before you make a final decision about a change, work with some of the staff who perform the work. This way you can learn the unintended consequences of your proposal. Shadowing helps you make a more informed decision and can increase staff buy-in for system changes by involving staff in the process.

BENEFITS TO THE SHADOWEE

Shadowing is a great way to encourage effective participation. Managers see firsthand what their staff members are dealing with on a day-to-day basis and get to know their staff members and their talents far better than what is casually observed by walking through a department or during staff meetings. The shadowee has an opportunity to spend several hours of one-on-one time with a library administrator to share their successes and frustrations.

SHADOWEES GET ONE-ON-ONE TIME WITH THE BOSS

Make sure shadowees understand the benefits of shadowing. Communicate the fact that this is an opportunity for staff members to have several hours of one-on-one time with a library administrator—a chance for the staff member to show the boss what's really going on!

There is a lot to be learned by listening to what frustrates your staff. As a manager, a large part of your job is to provide staff with the tools and training needed to be successful in their work. When I was shadowing Dan, the delivery driver, he mentioned how heavy the delivery bins were. This led to using permanent marker to draw a fill line on the inside of the delivery bins, a simple and inexpensive solution to a staff issue. Shadowing provides limitless opportunities to make small but beneficial changes in your organization.

42

STAFF SHORTAGES

Bradley Tolppanen and Janice Derr

SUCCESSFULLY OPERATING a library during a time of staff shortage is a significant challenge for library managers. A shortage in the number of staff members can result from, among other examples, hiring freezes, medical leaves, or military leaves. We have found that during a staff shortage the goal should always be to strive to maintain optimal services for the patrons regardless of problems behind the scenes with the staffing levels.

FILLING THE SHORTAGES

In cases where the shortage has been caused by reasons other than budget, the manager can investigate hiring new staff or assigning more hours to current staff. Explaining the impact of the shortage to the library's administration or library board could result in being allowed to hire more people or give out more hours. In general, shortages can be addressed through temporary employees, overtime, and volunteers.

Temporary Employees

If a staff member is expected to be away for several months, the library could hire a temporary employee, either full-time or part-time, to help cover the absence. A temporary employee may require significant training before getting fully up to speed and contributing, by which time the absent employee may be close to returning. To get the most from a temporary employee from day one, the manager should try to hire a person familiar with libraries. We had great success hiring a retired staff member back as a temporary employee, whereas hiring those without experience was less effective since they took much longer to train. The manager should work out duties for temporary employees that allow them to contribute at the earliest point in their employment. The simplest duties of an absent staff member could be assigned to the temporary employee, with more complicated tasks assigned to current members of the staff.

Overtime

Another method to cover the absence of a staff member, if funds are available, is to extend overtime to present full-time staff or give more hours to present part-timers. If the shortage persists over several months, however, the current staff could become burned out.

Volunteers

Recruiting volunteers can provide assistance in overcoming a shortage. Though enthusiastic and ready to help, volunteers are best used on the most basic tasks, such as shelving.

FOCUS ON ESSENTIAL TASKS

When you are trying to overcome a staff shortage, it is essential to maintain excellent patron service and achieve the core goals of the department. Customer service should never suffer. Shortages can be overcome by concentrating on the core duties. A core duty is one that needs to be done in order for patrons to use the library and access information resources—anything from opening the doors in the morning, to cataloging newly purchased materials, to maintaining the library website. Additionally, every department has duties that are not entirely necessary to the core mission, such as a shifting project in circulation or processing gift donations in acquisitions; these types of tasks can be tabled in times of shortages.

After determining the core duties as well as what tasks can be suspended or delayed, the library manager should assign the duties to the remaining staff members. Care should be taken to not give too much extra work to one person. The work should be distributed evenly throughout the department.

COOPERATION WITHIN THE LIBRARY

A focus on cooperation within the library helps make things run more smoothly during a shortage. In large institutions, cooperation could take place among departments; in smaller libraries, cooperation among the staff members is essential. Staff members from a fully staffed department can be loaned for all or part of their work day to assist the department that is operating below normal staffing levels. Such cooperation ensures that people are available to get the most important tasks done. Examples of such sharing: acquisitions staff assist with opening the library; cataloging staff cover lunch breaks at a circulation point; staff from circulation help out in cataloging. Assigning tasks to people from other departments has the bonus of generating a greater respect for the work being done by other people. Cross-training allows staff members to contribute outside their normal areas. Flexibility and an understanding of why cooperation is necessary are required on the part of the shared employee for such sharing to be successful.

REVIEWING WORKFLOW

A time of staff shortage is an excellent opportunity for the library manager to review thoroughly the workflow and the work processes being used by the staff. Take the time to do this positive step. It will be useful not only in the short term but in the future as well. You may find that there are quicker and easier ways of doing things or ways to apply technology that had previously been overlooked. A different staff member completing a task may discover a more efficient way to get the work done. As always, encourage staff members to bring their ideas forward to their supervisor. We have been able in the past to streamline the work of positions that had been unfilled. Outdated steps were removed from the workflow and technology was introduced to maximize efficiency. This streamlining allowed the work to be completed during the time of the shortage as well as when the position was filled. Implement these time-saving (and often money-saving) changes now.

STAFF MORALE

One thing that may suffer during a staff shortage is morale. Employees may be apprehensive about working with fewer people. They may worry that, even though they are working the same number of hours per week, they will have to take on significantly more work. As with most staffing issues, the most important principle is communication. Speak to staff and let them know the situation. Relay information as you receive it, and ask staff for their input. Keeping them in the loop makes them feel like part of the team. Even when busy, managers should take the time to listen to each comment and complaint. You may get some good suggestions. Making sure that everyone feels they are being heard keeps the lines of communication open. In what can be a stressful situation, the last thing a manager needs is an upset staff member.

Library managers should recognize the achievements of the people working for them. Showing appreciation for the staff during a trying and busy time raises morale. Be sure to let everyone know that you recognize their hard work and appreciate their willingness to pull together. A thank-you to someone working out of their normal area or taking on a new task shows an understanding of their efforts. No one expects you to throw a party, but who doesn't like cake.

The library manager should be available to help the staff get the work completed. From a morale point of view, it is important for the manager to be seen pitching in. Without a full staff, the manager should be available, for example, to come in early to open or help cover lunch breaks at a service desk. The manager should frequently check to make sure that tasks are being completed and help out as needed.

Staff shortages can be difficult times, but they need not have devastating effects on your library. If you as a library manager choose to think of them as a time to assess work flow and efficacy, the library may even come out of it better than before the shortage. And if you go into it willing to communicate with staff and roll up your sleeves and work along with them, you will probably create an even stronger department.

PART V
Public Relations

43

NO SURPRISES: KEEPING YOUR BOARD IN THE LOOP

Lynn Hawkins

AT MENTOR (Ohio) Public Library we conduct trustee communication with the "No Surprises" rule in mind. No board member wants to open the paper to read that the library is being picketed. Nor do trustees appreciate appearing uninformed about a state budget reduction in the face of media demands for information. Trustees do not like to appear uninformed and they certainly do not like to be uninformed—and who could blame them? They have been entrusted with making policy for a publicly funded organization. The public scrutiny that comes with the package can be uncomfortable for some in the best of cases and world-rocking (theirs) in the worst. This chapter provides some easy methods of communication to engage and inform your board.

What kind of information should you routinely forward to your trustees? Most of us would agree that there is rarely an "ordinary" day in library work. But new information on a critical issue or an incident outside the routine of your day should be shared with your trustees. Here are some examples:

- budget information of any kind from the county auditor, state auditor, state library, or library association lobbyists—with special attention to news regarding budget reductions both planned and speculative
- lawsuits, both threatened and filed
- accidents and your follow-up actions
- calls to action and advocacy alerts from state and regional library associations and library lobbyists
- incidents of note. If it warrants an incident report, a quick heads-up to the board is prudent in case of fallout.
- early/inclement weather closings; power outages
- security breaches. Did vandals trigger a police alarm last night? Let the board know.
- good news: grant awards and awards in general. Don't wait until the monthly board meeting—your board likes good news as much as you do.
- programs, both to encourage trustee attendance and to help them speak informatively as advocates
- public record requests. If the title of public records officer is part of your job description, you should keep your board routinely informed of requests for library public records.

- police reports. If you had to fill out a police report for theft, assault, public disturbance, or virtually anything else, it is of interest to the board.

JUST THE FACTS, MA'AM

Keeping the board informed is easier if you keep them engaged. So how should you keep your trustees engaged? The monthly report for board meeting packets is a great chronicle of your busy month, but what about all of that time between board meetings?

The weekly update is a great answer to this issue because it is a sound bite. Choose a day that works for your schedule; you might select Monday in order to review the entire previous week. Keep each month's weekly updates in a folder on your desktop and add to the report all week long so that it is ready to go on Monday. Your update should go out via e-mail as a list of bulleted items—quick to document, quick for trustees to read: just the facts, ma'am. Be sure to include a print copy as part of your monthly report in board packets so that it is part of the record. This is a great way to document both your hard work and the library's progress.

Give each trustee an e-mail account on your server. The best reason for this is that it is easy to keep track of e-mail, which is subject to the public records law. If you receive a public records request, the e-mail can be simply retrieved from your server. All library e-mail can auto-forward to trustees' personal accounts so that they do not have to check two accounts; just remind them to use the library account for all replies in order to protect their personal accounts from public record requirements.

If your library utilizes e-mail software such as Microsoft Exchange, consider creating a shared calendar. It is easy to "invite" trustees to a meeting. When they respond to the invitation, it appears on their calendars. If you prefer not to use a shared calendar, you can still e-mail trustees through Outlook and flag the list for reminders. Outlook automates the reminders for you.

COMMITTEE MEETING ANNOUNCEMENTS: Keep It Simple

Committee meetings can be advertised to the public and trustees routinely; we all need reminders to keep busy schedules straight. In some cases there are also notice requirements to be met for sunshine laws. Multiple meeting schedules can easily be memorialized for everyone if your library employs a web-based event calendar. This requires that each board committee determine meeting dates and times for the entire year at its annual organizational meeting. Getting the group to select that standard meeting time and place is the tricky part—the rest of the process is simple and you can accomplish it for them:

- Meeting dates and times are sent to the media and placed on the library's web-based event calendar.
- Each trustee is registered by you for event notifications.

- Each trustee automatically receives a reminder e-mail of the meeting.
- Some web calendars also permit users to download event information and a reminder request with a simple mouse click. This is the "fun and easy" part of your tutorial for your board.

TRACKING COMMITTEE PROGRESS AND ASSIGNMENTS: Agendas and Reports

With the exception of a retreat, work session, or emergency meeting, a standard agenda may be adopted for committee meetings. No need to reinvent the wheel for each agenda. Standard agenda items include approval of previous minutes, old business, and new business. Tailor the rest of the agenda to include two or three things the committee reviews routinely, like fundraising or condition of the physical plant.

Next, document progress on committee initiatives for the group with a committee report form. This form can also serve as a bulleted form of committee minutes. You may tailor the form to your library, but it should include basic items to keep everyone on the same page: committee's primary objectives (this should never be vague), action items, scheduled meetings, responsibilities and committee member assignments, and progress and target dates for each project. The committee report form can be filled out each time the committee meets, in this way both tracking and reporting progress and keeping individual members on task.

ROUTINE BOARD CALENDAR: Stuff We Do Year after Year

This may seem like a no-brainer, but because your board has turnover you need to update continually the collective consciousness regarding routine requirements so that everyone knows what is coming. The monthly routine board calendar ties to board bylaw requirements, state and local report deadlines, and such trigger dates as a date by which the health insurance carrier must be notified of changes. Examples of items for this calendar include these:

swearing-in of officers

quarterly budget review

annual report to state library

approval of payroll dates for following year

appointment of nominating committee for next year's officers

biennial state audit

committee assignments

goal setting for executive director

evaluation deadlines

appointment of legal counsel

As a final note, you might work with your board president in January to develop a "hotlist" of longer-term issues and projects that require attention during the coming year. Items for inclusion on this hotlist might be labor negotiations, strategic planning, purchase of property, or the search for a new board attorney or executive director. The hotlist assigns ownership to each project and is a simple way to touch base with the full board for progress on a quarterly basis. A checkmark in the "Completed" column is a real feel-good marker for all involved.

44

BOARD MEETINGS THAT WORK

James B. Casey

ONE OF the most difficult tasks confronting a new public library director is establishing a sound working relationship with the library board of trustees. Given the inevitable mix of personalities, local politics, and relationships long in place on the board before the arrival of the recently hired library director, there are not likely to be any firm and comprehensive rules for success that can prevent early termination or the gradual involvement by some trustees in the day-to-day operations of the library. Librarians can, however, take steps to seize the initiative in positive, nonconfrontational ways that can make board service more productive and enjoyable.

MEETING CONTENT AND THE DIVISION OF LABOR

One of the most important opportunities for such enhanced performance is in the preparation of content for regular and special board meetings. Avoiding lengthy discussion of minutiae and argumentation over how to address problems is essential for an effective meeting. A director needs to present clear, concise sets of recommendations and accompanying documentation. The board of trustees should not be expected to develop solutions to problems but to choose from a menu of recommendations developed by the library director and staff. Though board input can be extremely valuable and insightful, the nuts and bolts of implementation are matters of detail that need to be ironed out and presented to the board as recommendations. If the board declines to approve a given recommendation, the wise library director accepts that rejection and either perfects the solution or moves on to address other issues.

For example, in attempting to make corrections or improvements in a policy, the director needs to prepare a copy of the policy document with the various words struck out and the newly proposed language in bold. An accompanying memo explaining the need for wording changes might also help to clarify the intended improvement. If the changes are deemed to be unsatisfactory, a revised policy statement introduced in the next meeting with changes that reflect board concerns is preferable to a major rewrite during the meeting itself.

BUDGET MEETINGS

I recommend that in preparing annual budgets the director work in conjunction with staff over several weeks or months in advance of those board meeting dates where budget and levy approval are needed. The difficult chore of developing realistic revenue and budget projections that are reflective of the actual needs of the library is a task on which the director and staff must take the initiative. If the board has a designated subcommittee able to work with the director to offer general guidelines, this can be extremely helpful in the early stages of budget preparation. If the board has overall directives for the budget, the director needs to keep these in mind as the budget requests are being developed. The director can further expedite matters by developing a line-by-line analysis of each revenue and budget line that anticipates questions from trustees about projected changes over previous budgets. Detailed, advance preparation can often earn the confidence of board members and discourage the rewriting of budget lines by trustees.

PUBLIC MEETINGS

In addition to complying with state laws involving open-meetings notification, library directors need to take careful measures to assess the content of each and every agenda item as well as the accompanying documents for accuracy and clarity. Once the agenda has been discussed and agreed on with the board president, the agenda and accompanying material should be sent to all trustees several days in advance of the board meeting. Calling every trustee a day or two prior to the meeting to determine if there are any questions regarding the documents and agenda is strongly recommended. If there are questions or problems, the librarian has several days or hours to make corrections or to assemble information to address the question. Such prior interaction should help keep confusion and questions from slowing down the actual board meeting and creating the impression of disorganization during a public meeting.

CONSENT AGENDA

In addition to providing trustees with ample time to examine their materials well in advance of the board meeting, the next recommended step is to seek the adoption of a consent agenda. A consent agenda is, in effect, an agenda within the larger board meeting agenda. It lists regular agenda items that are necessary but routine and can be enacted in one motion. A consent agenda might include approval of minutes of the previous board meeting, bills and invoices, financial reports, lists of personnel

FIGURE 1. SAMPLE AGENDA, WITH CONSENT ITEMS

PUBLIC LIBRARY BOARD OF TRUSTEES
Regular Meeting—Tuesday, December 15, 2009, 7:00 p.m.

1. Call to Order and Roll Call
2. Pledge of Allegiance
3. Welcome to Visitors
4. Communications/Citizen/Staff Comments

CONSENT ITEMS (Items 5–9)
All items on the Consent Agenda are routine or have been brought forward at the direction of the Board of Trustees and will be enacted in one motion. If discussion is desired on any item, the item in question will be removed from the Consent Agenda and considered separately under New Business.

5. Approval of Minutes

   A. Special Meeting, November 17, 2009
   B. Regular Meeting, November 17, 2009

6. Bills and Invoices

   A. Library Materials, Check Numbers 22113–22164 . . . $44,890.28
   B. General, Check Numbers 22165–22218 . . . $40,269.12
   C. Manual, Check Numbers 5108–5138 . . . $88,841.91
   D. Report of Voided Checks

7. Financial Reports—Cash Report
8. Report of the Director—Personnel Changes
9. Policies Up for Review in December

   A. Conference and Membership for Trustees Policy
   B. Conference and Membership for Staff Policy
   C. Photographing and Videotaping in the Library Policy
   D. Board/Staff Committee Policy Statement
   E. Staff Association Policy
   F. Harassment Policy

END OF CONSENT AGENDA

10. Financial Reports

    A. Budget Fund Reports
       (i)   General Fund
       (ii)   Building Fund
       (iii) Working Cash Fund

11. Report of the Director

    A. Narrative Report
    B. Statistical Reports

12. Old Business

    A. Public Library Friends Report
    B. Committee Reports

C. Peer Jury Program
D. Library Foundation
E. Other

13. New Business

A. 2010 Building Fund Budget and Working Cash Fund
B. Approval of 2010 Salary Schedule
C. Proposed Revision of Personnel Policy/Benefit Levels Section
D. Library Board Meetings
E. Appointment of Freedom of Information Officer
F. Other

14. Adjournment

---

changes, and policies up for review where no changes have been recommended. The board president asks for a motion and second to approve the consent agenda. Trustees with questions or concerns about any item under the consent agenda can ask that the item be removed and placed under "New Business" for consideration. Once that is accomplished, every item remaining is approved automatically with the acceptance of the consent agenda. Figure 1 is an example of a board meeting agenda with "Consent Items."

More efficient board meetings can result in greater productivity, clearer focus on substantive issues, and less occasion for micromanagement and disputation. Preparation is the key.

45

LIBRARY PARTNERS: COOPERATING WITH OTHER NONPROFITS

John Helling

PUBLIC LIBRARIANS have long realized that the public library has become a point of access for many social services. Many librarians find themselves fielding reference questions that have little or nothing to do with the actual library. Patrons want to know where they can get tax help, which legal forms they need, or even where they can get a meal. Cultivating partnerships with other nonprofits is an essential part of appropriately responding to these types of requests. It is good to know that the AARP often offers free tax help to senior citizens, but it is even better to know that Bob Smith is the AARP point of contact at the local office. Making contacts and building partnerships at other nonprofits is a huge part of building the library's information referral capacity and can be a downright lifesaver for a small public library with limited resources.

ADVANTAGES OF PARTNERSHIP

One of the most frequent questions of this nature at the Bloomfield-Eastern Greene County (Indiana) Public Library is, "How do I get my GED?" Whenever this question is fielded, the librarians know exactly where to go. Since 1995, the offices of the Greene County Literacy Coalition have been located inside the library. The Literacy Coalition is a nonprofit organization, completely independent of the library, that provides one-on-one tutoring to adults in a variety of fields, such as GED preparation, English as a second language, adult literacy, and citizenship. Having this organization close at hand is invaluable. Patrons whom the librarians simply are not equipped to help are frequently referred to the Literacy Coalition. When a patron asks for a GED preparation book, or a book on teaching someone to read, it is often the case that the book itself does not address the root of the problem. In making the referral to the Literacy Coalition, the librarian is assuring that the patron will be getting more assistance than the book alone can provide.

In addition to providing it a space out of which to operate, the public libraries of Greene County partner with the Literacy Coalition in several other ways. Most directly, one former and three current area library directors serve on the Literacy Coalition's board of directors, ensuring that the local public libraries are directly involved in its operation and administration. This presence makes the public libraries aware of the educational needs of their patrons in a way that "normal" library service may not.

BOARD MEMBERSHIP: A FRONT-ROW SEAT

There is no better way to get to know an organization than to serve on its board. Volunteering to serve on the board of a local nonprofit gets you acquainted intimately with an organization and helps you identify the ways that organization could use the library's help to serve its target population.

The Bloomfield-Eastern Greene County Public Library and the Greene County Literacy Coalition also often partner on fundraising. Each organization knows that the other will provide fundraising help in many forms. The library opens its facilities for the Literacy Coalition's public fundraising events, and the Literacy Coalition offers letters of support for library grants. If the library receives more donations than its meager book sale storage area can handle, the excess goes to the Literacy Coalition, which then distributes them in exchange for donations at the local summer festival. Performing any of these activities as a single organization would be much more difficult than doing so with a partner.

The Literacy Coalition is also a collection development resource for the Bloomfield-Eastern Greene County Public Library. The Coalition coordinator is an excellent source for recommendations on adult literacy materials of all types, having first-hand experience with what works and what doesn't. She also has inside information on things that have an effect on the types of materials the library buys, such as the push to computerize the GED test. Having this resource close at hand is extremely convenient; it helps the library build an excellent adult literacy collection, which then has a direct and immediate impact on its target population, because the Literacy Coalition actively uses it.

STRATEGIES

Although it may not always be possible to permit another nonprofit to set up shop inside your building (even one with which your library is closely aligned), public libraries can still do much to cultivate useful partnerships.

The most direct way to form partnerships with other organizations is to get involved. Small, local nonprofits are almost always on the hunt for good board members. As a library director, your management experience and your position in the community are invaluable to small nonprofits, some of whom do not have a strong management structure and may struggle to make themselves known in the community. If you cannot make room in your hectic schedule to devote extra time to serving on yet another board, it is still worthwhile to make contact with the bigwigs in your area nonprofits. Local or regional meetings or conferences are a great place to make introductions. If you see an unrecognized face at the county nonprofit alliance meeting, or at a grantwriting workshop, or at a roundtable, take the time to introduce yourself and start networking.

IDENTIFYING HELPFUL PARTNERSHIPS

When targeting potential partners, it is a good idea to keep the library's mission in mind. Nonprofits with missions that align closely with that of the library are natural partners. What organizations within your community are already working alongside the library?

When you have begun networking and gotten to know your colleagues in the field, you can begin to make your needs known to one another. The library's strengths are usually its collection, its space, its public computers, and its staff. Can any of these be of use to another nonprofit? Does the other nonprofit know of a need that the library's print collection or public computer software fails to address? Conversely, other nonprofits can be useful to the library by providing programming and specialized information or services that librarians are often not trained to provide, such as GED tutoring and tax help.

Partners are also helpful when it comes time to raise funds. Many grants require letters of support, in-kind donations, and other evidence of cooperation. The library is often in a position to make some easy in-kind donations to the grant proposals of other nonprofits, such as use of library space, photocopies, and printing, which can be extremely helpful to smaller organizations that lack access to these amenities. In return, the library can hope to expect a letter of support from the partnering organization when it decides to write a grant proposal of its own. Having a preexisting network of other nonprofit managers is extremely useful when requirements like these arise.

No public library can do it alone. Partnerships are an essential way of keeping in touch with the community, broadening the reach of the library's collections and programming, and creating fundraising collaborations. With relatively little investment of time and effort, partnering with other nonprofits can lead to significant, invaluable gains for the library. Creating a network of colleagues who can be called on to pool resources with the library creates opportunities and benefits far beyond those outlined in this brief chapter.

46

PORTRAITS IN A SMALL TOWN: BALANCING ACCESS AND PRIVACY WITH A LOCAL HISTORY PHOTOGRAPHY COLLECTION

John Helling

WHEN YOU live in a small town, you get to know everyone. When you are the small town's only portrait photographer, you get pictures of everyone. If someone in Bloomfield, Indiana, got married, graduated from high school, had their picture taken for a church directory, or just took the family in for a nice photograph, chances are that Monty Howell took the picture. At the end of a twenty-year run, Monty Howell had a *lot* of pictures. Luckily for the Bloomfield-Eastern Greene County Public Library, Mr. Howell realized their historical value and asked the library if they would like to add his collection of photographic negatives to the local history collection.

Questions about genealogy and local history make up a large portion of the reference questions at small, rural public libraries, and Bloomfield-Eastern Greene County Public Library is no exception. The library fields requests from patrons for copies of obituaries, marriage records, birth records, cemetery records, and any other documentary evidence we can find of their long-dead relatives. Imagine if, fifty years from now, a genealogist contacted the library for a photocopy of a newspaper obituary and we were able to provide her with not only the usual black-and-white microfiche printout but a full-color photograph of her relative at her wedding. Needless to say, the library was excited about receiving this invaluable collection of photographs.

THINK BEFORE YOU LEAP: Obstacles

Enticing as the collection of photographs was, accepting this donation was less than straightforward. To begin with, Monty was a great photographer, but he was no cataloger. The negatives were grouped together by the first letter of the last name of their subject, but they were not alphabetized. Not even close. The negatives were also in need of a more permanent, archival housing if our genealogist of the future was going to be able to make use of them. Clearly, the library would have to devote some serious staff time to organizing, cataloging, and preserving this collection. With a small staff that already had plenty to do, finding room in the schedule to take a librarian off desk to work with the photos would be a challenge.

Privacy was also a big concern. Not only were the majority of the subjects in the photos still alive, they were still living in town and still coming into the library. Some of them might not be too happy to learn that a copy of their photograph was sitting in the library, waiting to be accessed by any old "researcher" who happened to request it. Several library board members also realized that they probably had photos buried in the collection as well. Clearly, the library needed to develop a privacy policy that would ensure that the collection could be used while respecting the privacy concerns of its patrons.

Additionally, we had to develop a method of access. For reasons concerning privacy, preservation, as well as practicality, the library did not want just any patron digging through the drawers of negatives. Some kind of finding aid was needed that would allow patrons to search the collection without harming the negatives or invading the privacy of others.

OVERCOMING THE OBSTACLES

Finding a way to allow staff the time to work on the project was the first hurdle. As any public librarian knows, free time for new projects is often in short supply. To help alleviate this situation, the library began advertising its project at Indiana University (a scant twenty miles away, in Bloomington), home to the School of Library and Information Science, in the hopes of attracting an intern or two. If successful, the library would receive some much-needed help at little or no financial cost, and the interns would receive on-the-job experience in cataloging, local history reference, and privacy issues. Once the library found some willing interns, they immediately began counting, sorting, and measuring the negatives. Any information gleaned from the negatives, such as any names or dates, was entered in a spreadsheet.

While these initial steps were being taken, the library director and the board set out to address the privacy concerns raised by the collection. Numerous sources were consulted, including the library's lawyer, the Indiana State Library, and other libraries with similar collections of photographs.

Legally, the library found itself on solid footing. The library's lawyer pointed out that because the original photographer owned the copyrights to the images and transferred them in writing to the library, the library was comfortably within its legal rights to use the photographs. He cautioned against being too free with them, however; mounting a display of photographs of people who could very well walk into the library on any given day, for example, might not be the wisest of public relations strategies. It was also his opinion that photographic records that could be used to identify patrons were no different than written records, as far as the law was concerned.

KNOW YOUR STATE REGULATIONS

The Indiana Code specifies that archival records that can be used to identify a patron can be distributed only to "qualified researchers, after the passing of a period of years that is specified in the documents under which the deposit or acquisition is made, or after the death of persons specified at the time of the acquisition or deposit." Check your state's code for similar language.

Since these photographs were of living, breathing residents of Bloomfield, privacy was a central concern. To help guard against misuse, the library developed a "Use of Photos" form from those of other libraries that stipulates that the photos may be used only for research and that the researcher assumes all responsibility for fair copyright use and invasion of privacy. The collection was also moved to an area where only staff could access it, to prevent unauthorized patrons from browsing the collection. To balance this privacy with the need for access, a search tool of some type had to be created. The small amount of metadata associated with the photos (surname of the subject, and very occasionally an age or date) had to be collected and mounted in such a way that patrons could search for what they needed but not be able to invade the privacy of others. In other words, the library had to let the researchers know what we had without letting them have direct, unfettered access to it.

LESSONS

The lessons we learned at the Bloomfield-Eastern Greene County Public Library were several:

Logistics. When accepting a new collection of this nature, a library should make sure that it has adequate resources to care for it. Rehousing several thousand photographic negatives into archival-quality housing is both time consuming and expensive. The library needs to be sure that it has accurately anticipated both of these costs.

Privacy. The library can expect to have patrons who are excited about the genealogical prospects of such a collection as well as patrons who are horrified that "anyone" has access to their photograph. Clear policies should be put in place to address who is allowed to use the collection and for what purpose.

Access. The library needs a way to ensure that the collection is usable while still regulating access. Placing the collection in a staff-only area is a good way to do the former, and assembling an index takes care of the latter.

Acquiring this collection of photographic negatives has been both a blessing and a curse for the Bloomfield-Eastern Greene County Public Library. Although we were thrilled to add such a complete snapshot in time of its populace to its local history collection, the library also had to take great care to ensure that the collection is handled with the appropriate care.

47

USING NUMBERS TO MAKE YOUR CASE

James B. Casey

AN OLD saying from the political realms of the nineteenth century gives humorous testimony concerning the persuasive value of numbers. "There are three kinds of lies: lies, damned lies, and statistics." Librarians need to give careful attention to the value of numbers in accentuating the value of their libraries and the services offered. Although many librarians enter the profession from a liberal arts background, the ability to use simple mathematics to quantify and justify what they do is becoming increasingly important as budgets come under more severe pressure.

Using percentages to highlight trends and accomplishments can be especially helpful. Determining percentages of increase or decrease is a fairly simple computation, but I am surprised at how many librarians either neglect to use such devices or are confused about how to undertake the calculation.

CALCULATING PERCENTAGE CHANGE

If your circulation went from 125,000 per year in 2009 to 135,000 in 2010, computing the percentage of increase is a simple matter of subtracting 125,000 from 135,000 and dividing the difference (10,000) by the earlier number (125,000) to show an 8 percent increase. If, on the other hand, your circulation went from 135,000 in 2009 down to 125,000 in 2010, the 10,000 is divided by the earlier number (135,000) for a decrease of 7.4 percent.

Naturally, library administrators want to accentuate positive trends by using statistics. If circulation is down or flat, there may well be other service measures on which you can focus. The number of persons attending library programs, logging into your Internet computers, presenting interlibrary loan requests, delivering hits on your library website, and even walking into your building can be extremely useful output measures indicating public demand for library services. If your attendance at preschool storytime increased from 75 to 91 during a given month over that same month one year earlier, reporting that as a 21 percent increase in participation may be more compelling than saying that sixteen more youngsters attended. When statistics indicate declining public interest in given collections, this can also prove to be a valuable management tool to signal the need to reassess expenditures or marketing efforts.

Sometimes it helps to look back in time to assess larger trends over a number of years. If the interlibrary loan requests placed by your residents increased from 5,000 during 2000 to 33,000 during 2009, the difference between the numbers (28,000) divided by the earlier number (5,000) would reveal a huge increase of 560 percent. Such a statistic can provide eloquent testimony to the rising public demand for library service and the growing success of its delivery over time. When such numbers show long-term decline, it may be less valuable for public discussion than as a compelling argument for management to consider a course correction.

Librarians also need to show local boards and decision-making bodies that they are delivering good value for a comparatively small amount of tax dollars received. In such cases, it may be less useful to emphasize that your total budget is one million dollars than to say that the budget increased by only 3 percent over the previous year. Although the average taxpayer may think that one million dollars is a huge sum of money, a 3 percent increase may not seem unreasonable. More important, libraries generally represent a relatively tiny percentage of the total tax bite the public must endure. Even what might seem like a big budget of five million dollars can be represented in light of tax bills to represent a small sum.

Examining a local property tax bill can be instructive if it has a breakdown of the amount and percentage charged for each tax-supported entity. If you divide the amount paid to the library by the total amount of the bill, you may be able to depict the cost of operating the library in favorable light, such as "Only 4 percent of the property taxes paid by residents of our municipality provides 95 percent of the revenue needed to run our library" or "The average home owner pays only $95 per year for our public library." The taxpayer might well use that dollar amount to consider that the cable television bill for one month or groceries for one week could represent a larger expense. If you are arguing for a new library addition or building, representing the total project cost of ten million dollars might be less helpful than saying that retirement of the bonds over twenty years would cost the average home owner only twelve dollars per year in additional taxes (for example).

Identifying the number of the library's current registered borrowers against the number of residents in the service area is another way of emphasizing the impact of library service on the community. If the number of registered borrowers is 35,000 and the total population of the service area is 55,000, you can say that 64 percent of the residents obtained a library card. If the percentage of active borrowers from the 35,000 can be identified, that would produce an even more compelling piece of evidence of service impact.

There are instances where comparing your library's expenditures with widely accepted resources such as the Public Library Data Service (PLDS) Statistical Reports can be particularly useful.[1] If you are challenged with arguments that the library pays too much for staff salaries, taking the total expenditure for salaries in the previous year and dividing that by the total expenditures for that year would give you the percentage devoted to salaries. If your expenditure for salaries is 50 percent and the PLDS Statistical Report for the year indicates that the average for public libraries of your size is 52.1 percent, this comparison could refute the charge that you are paying your staff too much. Similar state and regional salary guides could also provide valuable statistical evidence to refute or affirm arguments.

Sometimes a combination of output measures and expenditures can be persuasive. Not only can the often used statistic of cost per circulation be calculated by dividing the total expenditures of a library for a given year by the total circulation for that year, but other service measures such as questions answered, program attendance, hours of Internet access provided, community meeting room use, number of hits to databases and websites, and even visits to the library gathered from door counters can be used to quantify the value of services provided versus tax dollars expended. One can also determine the average cost of a book or DVD to calculate the amount taxpayers could save by borrowing such items from the library rather than making purchases.

There are times when percentages of increase or decrease can be less compelling than graphic or even physical depiction of numbers. If a library's summer reading program enrollment and number of participants are down from the prior year, setting up a display depicting the number of books read or number of hours devoted to reading can be an entertaining way of displaying the success of the program. A large wall mounting of paper circles, each representing one hour of reading completed by a youngster, or a display of thousands of ping pong balls, each representing a book read during the program, could demonstrate success more convincingly than percentages. Just saying that 1,200 youngsters enrolled in the reading program and read 35,000 books could be an impressive report apart from any reference to previous years.

Numbers do not always provide a fully accurate means of comparing the effectiveness of one library's performance against that of another. The higher circulation of one library may be offset by the higher number of reference inquiries or program attendance of another. Some communities tend to have more affluent or "upscale" clientele than others and may generate larger output measures. However, whatever the situation, there are always opportunities for librarians to employ statistics to identify trends and demonstrate the value of the services they provide.

Note

1. For the Public Library Data Service Statistical Reports, see www.ala.org/ala/mgrps/divs/pla/plapublications/pldsstatreport/index.cfm.

48

STAYING IN THE GAME: PUBLIC RELATIONS ON A SHOESTRING

Lynn Hawkins

WE LIBRARIANS buy books, pay our staff, and keep the buildings running. Often the last things for which we are able to budget are advertising and public relations. We want to be that third destination, but it is a challenge: people forget that we are here in the crush of advertising they encounter daily. As expenditures in shrinking budgets are carefully weighed, media money is harder to find. The good news is that there are inexpensive ways to raise our profiles both individually and collectively.

GREAT PRESS RELEASES

A properly drafted press release, built on a standard template, is your first tool for free media coverage. Be sure to send it two to four weeks ahead of the event date for editorial planning purposes. Guidelines for composing and submitting a low-maintenance press release include the following:

- Write a compelling headline.
- Text should include who, what, where, when, and why—two to three paragraphs, under 500 words.
- Report in the third-person.
- Use the Inverted Pyramid Model: important info at the top and least important info at the bottom; this is easier for an editor to edit.
- Provide accurate contact information.
- Include a quotation and Internet links, if appropriate.
- Send it to multiple editors: the community editor, the editor in chief.
- Call to check for receipt and offer to answer questions.
- Maintain a list of current media outlets and contact information for each.

THE MEDIA INTERVIEW: Be Ready

The second rule for getting good free publicity is to be ready to answer questions. Consider working with a preinterview checklist for both scheduled and unscheduled media interviews. At any given time there are predictable details about which you could be asked. Your preinterview checklist should include the following:

- your talking points (this is the interview you want to give)
- possible questions and your response in a sound bite
- worst possible question (this is the dreaded question you want to be ready for) and your response in a sound bite

NEWS FLASH: It Was News Only after It Happened

Many staffers involved in programming activities share a sense of entitlement regarding free print media publicity. It is worthwhile to remember that the media are not there to be your publicity agents; rather, they are there to report the news. The upcoming children's program on the library lawn, even if it will include live unicorns as entertainment, is *not news*. When the story and photos show up after the event, don't ask why the newspaper did not run the story before the event to publicize it. It was news only after it happened. That story may not have garnered free event publicity, but it is now free public relations. Accept it gratefully and leverage it whenever possible.

BEYOND FLYERS, BROCHURES, AND POSTERS: Blast It

Consider investing in software or assistance to create an e-mail list from your patron database. This is an inexpensive way to blast your newsletter, a link to an online survey you have posted, or a call-to-action for letters to state legislators. Your newsletter is your best public relations tool on a month-to-month basis, but postage for snail mail can be prohibitive. Once you have established an e-mail list service, you are good to go for virtually no cost. Remember that it is good practice to add an opt-out option for recipients who prefer not to receive such e-mail.

Does your local chamber of commerce do monthly e-mail blasts to members? What a great opportunity to highlight a standout program or new service to a different group. Ask the chamber if you can include one program a month in its e-mail blast.

BORROW OR RENT SPACE

Local hospitals, community centers, schools, businesses, city hall, the courts, and doctors' offices are all promising sites for library services, even if those services amount to just providing gently used books for borrowing or keeping. These are potential partnerships that should not be overlooked. Many of these potential partners also distribute their own newsletters. Ask for a column or paragraph to attract new patrons.

Another high-yield prime retail space worth considering is the local mall or grocery chain store. Look into the cost of placing a three- or four-sided pamphlet kiosk at either venue. Dedicate one side to library programming, one side to seasonal topics like tax forms or travel information, and one side to Friends of the Library news—and then ask the Friends to fund the kiosk. Your local mall is likely to provide a nonprofit rate, and you should negotiate down from that rate. The grocery chain may provide this space at no cost to the library. These are outstanding high-traffic venues for the library and worth every penny invested.

PARTNER, PARTNER, PARTNER

Every time you partner with another community organization or local business, you increase your advertising and public relations reach exponentially. If you partner with a local restaurant for an event or fundraiser, ask whether you can routinely make program information available in the form of mini-tabletop fliers. Your partnerships qualify as news, and they stand a great chance of free media coverage. When Mentor Public Library (Ohio) partners with Yours Truly Restaurants for "Dinner with the Presidents," it is front page above the fold, even though it is an annual event. When the library partners with the city's Parks and Recreation Department for "Storytime @ the Pools," the upcoming event descriptions make it into the city's program brochure that is distributed to every household in the city.

IT'S A TEAM THING

The best publicity of all is community involvement. Encourage every member of your staff to be involved with community service organizations and committee work. Provide for release time for this purpose whenever you are able. Management team members should be the long arms into the library district for that important community connection. Each member of the staff should appreciate that it is critical that they promote library services within the community. They are essential members of the marketing team for your library.

Friends of the Library are also important members of the marketing team. They can provide you with access to no-cost publicity through their newsletter, and the library can make a splash at every Friends book sale with a booth, table, and materials.

HOW'S THAT WORKING FOR YOU?

Maximize your public relations efforts by measuring success and continuing only those efforts that yield a positive return on investment. Consider maintaining a spreadsheet on your server's share drive or your library wiki. Each staff member responsible for press releases should track the following on the spreadsheet:

- potential publicity opportunities, including programs, new services, changes in hours, staff accomplishments, awards and honors, and anything that is news
- individual media outlets notified and notification dates for each
- dates of the successful publicity products

You may want to consider tracking these for an extended period to determine trends and successful outcomes of public relations efforts. Then you can arrange a meeting with your local media outlets to ask their advice on how best to arrange for news coverage. You will be armed with data that you should not use for diplomacy's sake, but you will also be armed with data that you can and should use internally to increase your success rate.

CONTRIBUTORS

Kris Baughman received her MA in library science from the University of Missouri, Columbia. She has taught middle school and high school and was the circulation department supervisor at Rockhurst University, in Kansas City, before becoming an elementary school media specialist with the Raytown, Missouri, C-2 School District. Kris is a member of the Missouri Association of School Librarians and the Greater Kansas City Association of School Librarians, for which she chairs the KC3 Reading Award Program for third-grade students in the Kansas City area.

Kim Becnel is juvenile services coordinator for Union County Public Library in Monroe, North Carolina. She holds an MLIS and PhD from the University of South Carolina at Columbia. Kim has a personal essay in *Contemporary American Women: Our Defining Passages* (ATTMP, 2009) and has authored several volumes in Bloom's How to Write about Literature series (2008–2011) and *The Rise of Corporate Publishing and Its Effects on Authorship in Early Twentieth Century America* (Routledge, 2007). Kim also contributed chapters to *The Frugal Librarian: Thriving in Tough Economic Times* (ALA, 2011).

Sian Brannon is technical services manager for the Denton Public Library, Denton, Texas, where she is responsible for technology, systems, interlibrary loan, statistics, acquisitions, cataloging, and circulation for the entire system. Sian believes there is a big difference between good managers and good supervisors. She is working on her PhD at Texas Woman's University with an emphasis in public library statistics.

James B. Casey has been director of the Oak Lawn Public Library, Chicago, since 1992. He holds a PhD in librarianship from Case Western Reserve University, MLS from SUNY Geneseo, and MA in history from Cleveland State University. He has worked in public libraries since 1973, served four terms on the ALA Council, and received the Librarian of the Year award from the Illinois Library Association in 2005.

Melissa J. Clapp is coordinator of instruction and outreach at Humanities and Social Sciences Library West, University of Florida in Gainesville. She earned an MA in English from Northern Illinois University and an MS in information studies from Florida State University. Melissa joined the University of Florida faculty in

2006, where she now coordinates the university library's mentoring program with the University Writing Program, working closely with the dean of students office in library outreach.

Janice Derr is a circulation librarian at Booth Library, Eastern Illinois University in Charleston. She has an MLS from the University of Missouri–Columbia and an MA in English from Eastern Illinois University. Previously she worked in reference services at Stephens College in Columbia, Missouri. Janice has presented at conferences in Illinois on a variety of topics, including interlibrary loan use patterns, student worker performance in access services departments, and creating successful freshman orientation programs, and she has published in the *Journal of Access Services*.

Barbara Fiehn is assistant professor of library media education at Western Kentucky University. She earned her EdD from St. Mary's University of Minnesota. After thirty years as a school librarian, library consultant, and media services coordinator, Barbara taught in library media education programs at Northern Illinois University and the University of Minnesota at Mankato. She has published a series of library automation articles in *Multimedia and Internet@schools* and "TQM-Continuous Improvement in the School Library Media Center" in *Educational Media and Technology Yearbook*. A member of ALA, Barbara serves on the Intellectual Freedom committee.

Holly Flynn is the mathematics/statistics librarian at Michigan State University in East Lansing, Michigan. Since earning her MLIS from Wayne State University in Detroit, she has published in the *Journal of Library Administration* and the online component of *Library Journal*. As a member of the Michigan Library Association, Holly leads a pilot Community of Practice on work/life balance issues for librarian/ parents. She is also a member of the Special Libraries Association, where she has presented on the value of creating job manuals.

Jeffrey A. Franks has been associate professor and head of reference at Bierce Library, University of Akron, Ohio, since 1995. He obtained his MLS from Kent State University. Jeffrey is a member of ALA and the Academic Library Association of Ohio. His publications, which reflect his acute interest in innovative reference models and learning commons, have appeared in *E-JASL (Electronic Journal of Academic and Special Librarianship), Reference Librarian, Journal of Educational Media*, and *Library Science*.

Michael Germano is the library faculty member at California State University, Los Angeles, dedicated to the College of Business and Economics, with a primary focus on teaching courses in financial information literacy as well as business information for decision making. He holds a law degree from Temple University and a master's degree in information science from Simmons College as well as an MA in English from New York University. Prior to joining California State's faculty, he worked at LexisNexis in a variety of sales and marketing positions.

Vera Gubnitskaia is youth services manager at Orange County Library System, Orlando, Florida. She obtained her library degrees from the Moscow Institute of Culture (Russia) and Florida State University. Vera has worked as a librarian, a manager, and a library consultant in public and academic libraries. Her articles describing community partnerships with public schools and Head Start groups appear in *Librarians as Community Partners: An Outreach Handbook* (ALA, 2010). Vera has presented at several conferences, including the Florida Library Association and Florida Literacy conferences. She is on the Florida Library Association Awards Committee.

Colleen S. Harris is associate head of access and delivery services at the North Carolina State University Libraries in Raleigh. She holds an MSLS from the University of Kentucky and an MFA in writing from Spalding University. Colleen prides herself on motivating library staff to excel at providing public service. She has published extensively on library management and staff development and has presented at ALA, Internet Librarian, and Computers in Libraries meetings. Her book *Development on a Budget: A Practical Guide for Librarians* is expected from Chandos in 2011.

Lynn Hawkins is executive director of the Mentor Public Library on the shores of Lake Erie, Ohio, the 2010 Mentor Chamber's Organization of the Year. She obtained her MLS from Kent State University. Lynn is coauthor of *High Tech, High Touch: Library Customer Service through Technology* (ALA, 2003) and author of numerous articles on library collaborations and board-director relationships. She has also presented at state and national library conferences. During her tenure as director of the Mooresville Public Library in Indiana, the library received the 2004 Outstanding Indiana Library Award.

John Helling is director of the Bloomfield-Eastern Greene County Public Library in Bloomfield, Indiana, and president of the board of directors of the Greene County Literacy Coalition. Previously he was a senior librarian at the Aguilar branch of the New York Public Library. John obtained an MLS from Indiana University, where he currently teaches a course in public library management. He has published an article and numerous book reviews in *Library Journal*.

Suzann Holland is director of the Monroe Public Library in Wisconsin. She earned both an MLIS and an MA in history from the University of Wisconsin–Milwaukee. Her previous writings have appeared in *VOYA*, *Public Libraries* (2010 Winner of *Public Libraries* Feature Award), *The PLA Reader for Public Library Directors and Managers* (Neal-Schuman, 2009), and *Local and Regional Government Information* (Greenwood Press, 2005). Suzann is currently working with the permission of the Laura Ingalls Wilder Estate on her first solo book, *The Little House Literary Companion*.

Susan Jennings is an assistant professor and lead desk services librarian in the Belk Library and Information Commons at Appalachian State University in Boone, North Carolina. She holds an MS in information science from the University of Tennessee at Knoxville and a BA and MA in history from Appalachian State University. Susan has worked in academic libraries for almost eighteen years. Her honors include being in the 2010 class of ALA's Emerging Leaders Program. Susan has published articles in *Tennessee Libraries*.

Ken Johnson is an assistant professor and coordinator of the learning and research services team in the Belk Library and Information Commons at Appalachian State University in Boone, North Carolina. He holds an MLIS degree from the University of North Carolina, Greensboro, and an MBA from Appalachian State University. Ken has served as team coordinator since 2008 and has ten years' experience as a business librarian at Drexel University and Appalachian State. He has published articles and book reviews in the *Journal of Business and Finance Librarianship*.

Jason Kuhl is manager of information services at the Arlington Heights Memorial Library in Arlington Heights, Illinois. He received his MS in library and information science from the University of Illinois and is a member of the ALA and Illinois Library Association. Prior to accepting his current position, he held various branch management positions with the St. Louis County (Missouri) Library. Ken actively seeks innovative ways to promote library services in his community, once even incorporating a raccoon puppet into a Rotary Club presentation.

Terry Ann Lawler is an assistant manager/children's librarian at the Phoenix Public Library, at the Palo Verde branch since 2008. She obtained her MLIS from the University of Arizona. Terry Ann is a member of the ALA and PLA. She has reviewed many books, audiobooks, and educational DVDs for *Library Journal* and *School Library Journal*. Terry has designed and presented programs at PLA, the Oregon Library Association, and Phoenix Public Library and has been recognized locally and nationally for her work with children and disconnected youth.

Erin O'Toole has been graduate library assistant coordinator at the University of North Texas Libraries, Denton, since 2004. She obtained her MLS from Texas Woman's University and is a member of ALA and the Texas Library Association. Erin's writings have appeared in *Public Libraries* and *Public Library Quarterly*, and she contributed to *Encyclopedia of Time: Science, Philosophy, Theology, and Culture* (Sage, 2009). She is a science reviewer for *Educational Media Reviews Online* and a frequent presenter on the topics of science fair reference and collection development for school and public libraries.

Rebecca Marcum Parker earned her bachelor's degree in English and library science education and MA in literature from the University of Central Missouri. Formerly a bookmobile librarian, she has twelve years' experience as an inner-city school librarian, currently at Satchel Paige School in the Kansas City, Missouri, School District. She is a member of the Isak Federman Teaching Cadre of the Midwest Center for

Holocaust Education, the Missouri Association for School Librarians, and the Greater Kansas City Association of School Librarians. She is a *Kansas City Star* columnist.

Alice B. Ruleman is access services librarian and assistant professor of library science at James C. Kirkpatrick Library, University of Central Missouri in Warrensburg. She obtained her MLS from Emporia State University and is currently working on an MS in educational technology. Alice is active in the Missouri Library Association and MOBIUS. She has served as director-at-large and is currently the vice president of the board of the Association of Christian Librarians and is on the editorial team of the journal *Christian Librarian.*

Seamus Scanlon is the librarian of the Center for Worker Education— the downtown campus of City College of New York. He holds a first-class honors BS from University College Galway, a library science master's from Thames Valley University, London, and an MFA from the City College of New York. He previously worked in universities in Cambridge, Southampton, Belfast, and Galway. For his work at the Center for Worker Education he won a 2009 I Love My Librarian Award sponsored by the Carnegie Corporation and *New York Times.*

Robin Shader is the deputy director of Chattahoochee Valley Libraries, headquartered in Columbus, Georgia. She obtained her MLS from Rutgers University and has published articles in *School Library Journal,* ALA APA's *Library Worklife,* and the ALA Learning Round Table newsletter, *LearningExchange.* Robin is a member of ALA, PLA, LLAMA, ALA Learning, and the Georgia Library Association. She is a 2003 graduate of the New Jersey Library Association's Emerging Leaders program. She is currently facilitating a leadership program called CVL Leads! to grow and inspire the next generation of library leaders.

Roxanne Myers Spencer is associate professor and coordinator of Western Kentucky University Libraries' Educational Resources Center. She teaches collection management as an adjunct in WKU's Library Media Education. Roxanne earned an MSLS from Clarion University of Pennsylvania and an MAEd from Western Kentucky University. From 2004 to 2008 she was involved in an international school library exchange project with a private P–12 school near Barcelona, Spain, which led to her article "Developing Library Classroom Children's Collections in English for a Catalunyan Private School" in *Collection Building.* Roxanne reviews young adult fiction, nonfiction, and multimedia for *School Library Journal.*

Geoffrey P. Timms has been electronic resources/web/systems support librarian at Mercer University's Jack Tarver Library, Macon, Georgia, since 2007. He received his MLIS from the University of South Carolina. Geoff is a member of ALA and ACRL. His work has appeared in *Georgia Library Quarterly* and *Journal of Electronic Resources Librarianship,* and he has presented on managing access to e-resources at

ALA Midwinter and the Charleston Conference in 2009. Geoff is currently working on streamlining and semi-automating periodical evaluations.

Bradley P. Tolppanen is the head of circulation services at Booth Library, Eastern Illinois University. Previously he held positions in reference services at the University of Louisiana, Monroe, and the Northern Alberta Institute of Technology. Bradley holds an MLIS from the University of Alberta and a master's degree in history from the University of New Brunswick. He has presented at library conferences in Illinois and has been published in the *Journal of Access Services, Internet Reference Services Quarterly*, and *Louisiana Libraries*.

Lorette S. J. Weldon has been special library association project archivist, University of Maryland Baltimore County, since 2008. She obtained her MLS from the University of Maryland. Lorette has been webinar instructor and *Board Professionals Newsletter* editor for Association of Governing Boards of Universities and Colleges and *Records Manager Newsletter* editor for the Society of American Archivists. She has articles in *Computers in Libraries, Information Outlook,* and the Association of Governing Boards of Universities and Colleges' *Trusteeship* and has been a speaker at the Special Libraries Association 2009 and Computers in Libraries 2009 and 2010 conferences.

Kimberly Wells is assistant manager and circulation supervisor at the South branch of the Denton Public Library, Denton, Texas. She received her MLS from the University of North Texas and spent six years as a genealogy librarian at the Fort Worth Public Library. She currently serves on the ALA Reading List Committee and the Texas Library Association Lariat Task Force.

Ashanti L. White is an Academic and Cultural Enrichment Scholar pursuing her master's in library and information systems at the University of North Carolina at Greensboro. She has more than seven years' experience in public and academic libraries. She previously earned a BA in political science and African American studies with a minor in philosophy and an MA in liberal studies with a concentration in world cultures. Her works have appeared in *Black Enterprise, Third Wednesday*, and *Mandala Literary Journal* among other publications.

INDEX

software mentioned
  Adobe Acrobat Connect Pro, 7
  for blogs, 83
  Confluence wiki software, 100
  CybraryN session control software,
    105–106
  DeskTracker (for keeping statistics), 6
  Google Apps suite, 85–88
  MediaWiki, 111–112
  Microsoft Excel, 20, 60, 90, 103
  Microsoft Exchange, 156
  Microsoft Office, 120
  Microsoft Outlook, 60, 156
  PBworks wiki software, 100–101, 111
  PowerPoint presentations, 68
  publishing programs, use of, 61–62
  Statistical Package for the Social
    Sciences, 55
  text expansion programs, 86
  wiki applications, 112
  Wimba collaboration service, 131
  See also spreadsheets, use of
solo librarians
  attracting volunteers, 39
  managing more than one library, 60–62
  in school libraries, 56–59
Spencer, Roxanne Myers, 37–40, 72–75,
  179
spreadsheets, use of
  cataloging local history collections, 166
  computer inventory, 23
  public relations, 173
  scheduling, 60, 101, 103
  staff accountability system, 20
  support, 90
  tracking users with overdues, 26
Springboard course management system, 89
staff
  accountability system for, 19–21
  blogs for, 83
  and change, 144
  delegation of tasks to, 86–87
  generational differences, 117–119
  for overnight services, 58
  parents on, 127–129
  part-time staff, 49, 128
  personal production capacity of, 23
  as promoters of library, 173

  at satellite libraries, 25
  scheduling of, 60, 87, 101, 128, 129
  See also meetings with staff; staff training
staff, communication with
  in branch libraries, 31–33
  and change, 144
  electronic message boards, 28
  during emergencies, 17, 124–125
  and Facebook, 79–81, 107–109
  graduate assistants, 123
  and managing more than one library,
    60–61
  and shadowing, 146–148
  and SharePoint, 92–99
  during staff shortages, 151
  student assistants, 79–81
staff shortages, xiii, 149–151
"Staff Shortages" (Tolppanen and Derr),
  149–151
staff training
  on diversity, 14
  emergencies, 126–127
  graduate assistants, 121–122
  on harassment and disability
    compliance, 13
  for IT support, 91
  leadership training, 49–53
  for library instruction programs, 67–68
  for merging service points, 65
  new employees, 135–136
  peer-to-peer training, 118
  temporary employees, 149
  See also cross-training; manuals
stakeholders
  in managing overnight hours, 57
  in merging service points, 63
Statistical Package for the Social Sciences,
  55
statistics
  in promotion of library, 168–170
  in staff accountability system, 20–21
"Staying in the Game" (Hawkins), 171–173
stress management, xiii
student assistants
  communication with, 79–81
  for IT support, 90
  See also graduate assistants
student-centric library service, 53–56

You may also be interested in

LIBRARIANS AS COMMUNITY PARTNERS
EDITED BY CAROL SMALLWOOD
Edited by Carol Smallwood

Including 66 focused snapshots of outreach in action, this resource reflects the creative solutions of librarians searching for new and innovative ways to build programs that meet customer needs while expanding the library's scope into the community.

PRINT ISBN: 978-0-8389-1006-1
204 PAGES / 6" X 9"

MORE BOOKS EDITED BY CAROL SMALLWOOD

THE FRUGAL LIBRARIAN
ISBN: 978-0-8389-1075-7

PRE- AND POST-RETIREMENT TIPS FOR LIBRARIANS
ISBN: 978-0-8389-1120-4

WRITING AND PUBLISHING
ISBN: 978-0-8389-0996-6

MORE BOOKS ON LIBRARY ADMINISTRATION AND MANAGEMENT

BE A GREAT BOSS
CATHERINE HAKALA-AUSPERK
ISBN: 978-0-8389-1068-9

THE CHALLENGE OF LIBRARY MANAGEMENT
WYOMA VANDUINKERKEN AND PIXEY ANNE MOSLEY
ISBN: 978-0-8389-1102-0

ORGANIZATIONAL STORYTELLING FOR LIBRARIANS
KATE MAREK
ISBN: 978-0-8389-1079-5

Order today at **alastore.ala.org** or **866-746-7252!**
ALA Store purchases fund advocacy, awareness, and accreditation programs for library professionals worldwide.

9 780838 911211